An Anthology of
DECORATED
PAPERS

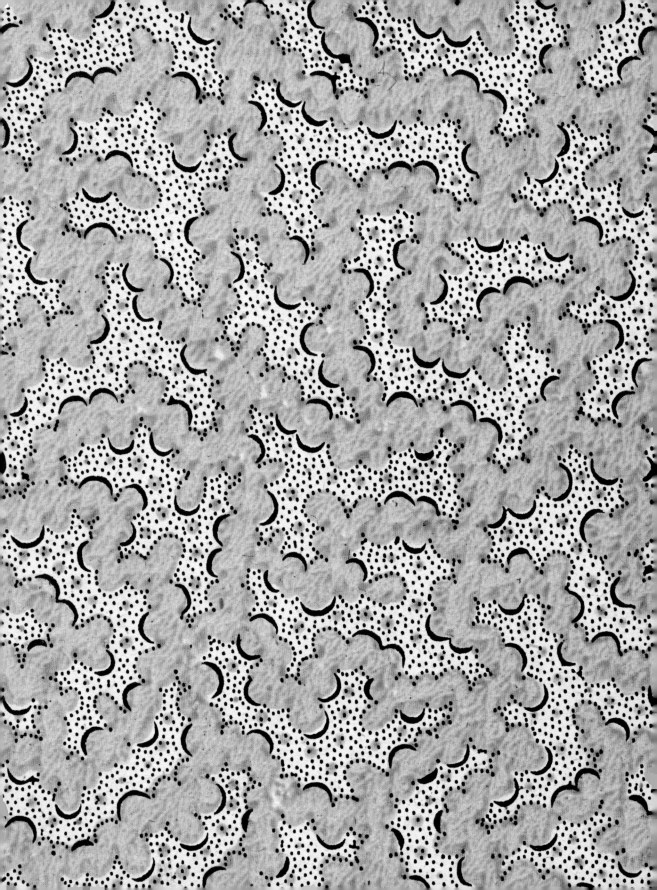

P.J.M. Marks

An Anthology of

DECORATED PAPERS

A Sourcebook for Designers

Cover
The decorated papers that appear on the cover can be found on the following pages: (front) 160, 2; (spine) 26; (back) 165, 174–75.

Frontispiece
Late eighteenth- to early nineteenth-century European block printing. The sense of movement and cheerful colours are characteristic of this type of paper. J.686

Page 6
Twentieth-century American paper by the influential collector Rosamond B. Loring (1889–1950). Loring's notebook, published as *Marbled and Paste Papers* (2007), includes instructions for mixing paste paint. Many of today's practitioners, however, prefer to formulate their own recipes. J.2576

Page 8
Twentieth-century stylized version of *hatip ebru* inspired by traditional Turkish marbling. J.1979

Page 20
Eighteenth-century European marbling. J.1675

Page 62
Twentieth-century European paste paper with veining. J.2589

Page 98
Eighteenth-century German brocade paper by Johann Michael Schwibecher of Augsburg, Germany. J.136

Page 132
Nineteenth- to twentieth-century block print, probably Chinese. J.3466

Page 170
Twentieth-century European block print. J.3519

Page 204
Probably early twentieth-century European monochrome paper with embossing in black. Cut in positive relief, the pattern gives the paper's surface a tactile quality. J.3076

For Patricia Bettis, my mother

First published in the United Kingdom in 2015 by
Thames & Hudson Ltd, 181A High Holborn, London WC1V 7QX

in association with

The British Library, 96 Euston Road, London NW1 2DB

This compact edition first published in 2018

An Anthology of Decorated Papers: A Sourcebook for Designers
Text and illustrations © 2015 The British Library; for exceptions, see page 256
Design and layout © 2015 Thames & Hudson Ltd, London

British Library Cataloguing-in-Publication Data
A catalogue record for this book is available from the British Library
ISBN 978-0-500-29392-8

Printed and bound in China by Toppan Leefung

To find out about all our publications, please visit
www.thamesandhudson.com. There you can subscribe
to our e-newsletter, browse or download our current catalogue,
and buy any titles that are in print.

ACKNOWLEDGMENTS

Thanks are due to my colleague and friend Gill Ridgley (ex-LSE), whose sound historical sense and editing skills have helped portray occasionally disparate matters more concisely.

This book could not have been written without the support of Head of Printed Heritage Collections Adrian Edwards and many other British Library colleagues. I am fortunate to work with them on such amazing collections. My genial and kind manager, John Goldfinch, has neatened prose, improved structure and, together with colleagues Iris O'Brien, Greg Smith and Alessandra Panzanelli, provided tea and sympathy.

I have benefited considerably from paper-decorator and researcher Susanne Krause's unusual combination of practical and theoretical skills. She has helped me reconsider traditional views and not just reproduce received wisdom. Her work clarifying international terminology and providing a focus for the cooperation of European decorated-paper collections has been invaluable. I only hope that helping me has not hampered work in her studio.

Researchers into paper decoration are generous and engaging. With their dedication and forensic knowledge of techniques, Julia Rinck and Matthias Hageböck have provided much-needed direction.

I am grateful to Mirjam Foot, who has laid the foundations for research on the Olga Hirsch collection, and to Karen Limper-Herz, Emilie Fissier and Philippe Munsch for uncovering the more obscure sources of decorated-paper information. Colleagues Richard Morel, Malini Roy and Ursula Sims-Williams have been generous in sharing their knowledge of the British Library's India Office, Visual Arts, and Asian and African Studies collections, locating hidden papers.

The Olga Hirsch collection remains alive thanks to the generosity of artists and collectors, including Sandy Cockerell, Compton Marbling, Graham Day, Marie-Ange Doizy, Victoria Hall, Rose Issa, Yeong-Yon Kim, Susanne Krause, Claire Maziarczyk, Izhar Neumann, Virginia Passaglia, Gisela Reschke, Hans and Tanya Schmoller and Richard J. Wolfe, whose donations provide a perspective on what went before. The many researchers of the collection, notably Claire Prince, have helped increase my own understanding of the subject.

The Schmoller collection of decorated papers at Manchester Metropolitan University, the online images of the collection and the staff of the university's Special Collections department have proved a vital resource.

The many others who deserve appreciation include Kristian Jensen, whose scholarship and support I respect and value. I must also remember to say hello to Jason Isaacs, and to express gratitude for the steadfast encouragement of Angela Forester, Kady Milne, Anne Barrett Rainford, Sharon Eckman and Wan Lan Sng.

The composure of Robert Davies, managing editor at the British Library, has been remarkable – and necessary. Thank you, too, to Thames & Hudson, whose editors and designers have made many valuable suggestions, and whose guidance is reflected in every aspect of this book.

P.J.M. Marks

9 INTRODUCTION

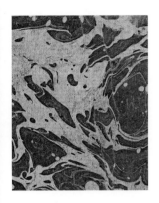

21
HAND-
MARBLED
PAPERS

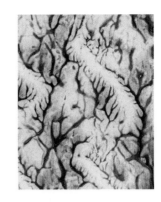

63
PASTE
PAPERS

99
BROCADE
PAPERS

133
BLOCK-
PRINTED
PAPERS

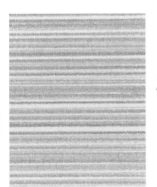

171
MASS
PRODUCTION
The Nineteenth Century
and Beyond

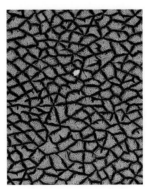

205
MISCELLANEOUS
DECORATING
TECHNIQUES

250 NOTES
252 GLOSSARY
253 FURTHER READING
255 INDEX

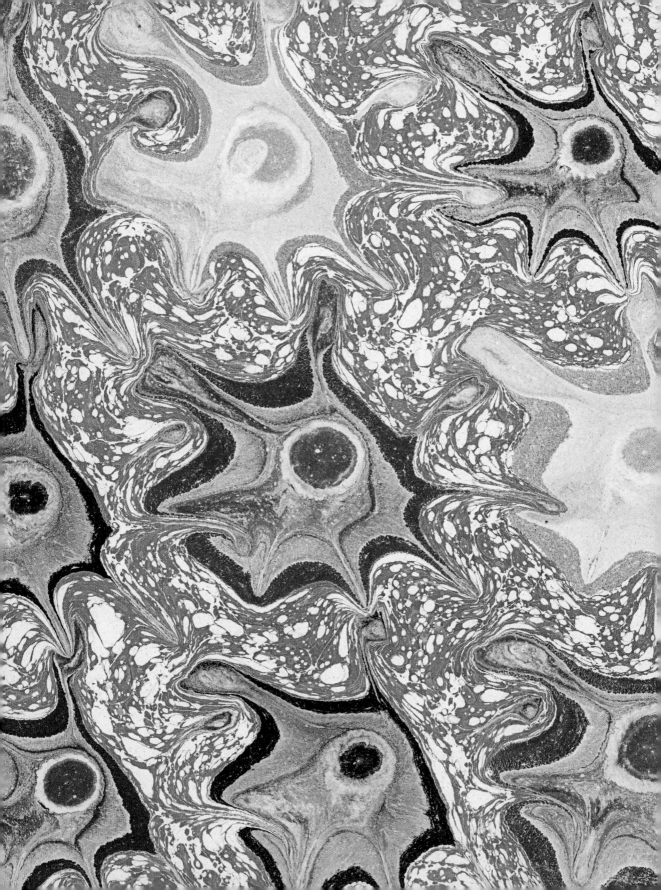

INTRODUCTION

Patterns are to be found everywhere, yet they often go unnoticed: the intricate framework of veins on a leaf; some colourfully printed food wrapping. If such things pass unobserved, can they be significant? Moreover, the terms 'decoration' and 'pattern' are not usually associated with high art, so why are decorated papers important?

The decorated papers under discussion here consist of thin, flexible, ornamented sheets used for a variety of different purposes. The majority were inexpensively produced and not required to be enduring works of art (although there are some exceptions). They tended to be produced in bulk using either a single method or a number of methods combined. This introduction, the aim of which is to provide some historical context, is followed by chapters devoted to the major decorating techniques (marbling, block printing, brocade, paste, industrial, miscellaneous) and images of the papers themselves.

Most of the featured papers belong to the Olga Hirsch collection at the British Library. A trained bookbinder, Mrs Hirsch (1889–1968) gathered and catalogued decorated papers after discovering them covering scores in the library of her music-collector husband. Little formal research had been done on the subject until 1961, the publication date of Albert Haemmerle's *Buntpapier*, which was based on the Olga Hirsch collection among others. The papers in the collection number some 3,500 but cannot, of course,

provide an example of every interesting paper ever made. Not all nations in which papers were used are included in this book, notably Spain, while some, such as the Low Countries, are sparsely represented.[1]

The papers showcased here provide examples of decorating techniques that have been practised throughout the world for hundreds of years. No universally accepted terminology for their description has yet emerged, although there are useful manuals, not least *Decorated Paper: A Guide Book* (2009). Terms can mislead, however, particularly the one used to describe a range of eighteenth-century German brocade papers, 'Dutch gilt', which is either a misinterpretation of the word 'Deutsch' or a reference to the Netherlands, which organized the export of such papers. The same terms are not used in every country (not every region uses every technique), nor do they coincide exactly in different countries or at different periods. In France, the term 'papier décoré' may refer to block-printed papers or to all decorated papers as a category (including marbled and brocade). 'Papiers dominotés' (a term whose origin is unclear) usually refers to sheets block-printed with geometric designs or repeated motifs.[2] In Germany, the equivalent all-embracing term would be 'Buntpapier'.

The different styles of marbling can be particularly difficult to understand. Some can be so similar only a professional would be able to distinguish them, especially 'bouquet' and 'peacock'. Moreover, terms do not always describe the pattern. 'Spanish marbling', for example, refers to a pattern made by the paper being moved in a particular way, resulting in a series of 'waves', near-parallel straight lines lying diagonally.[3]

The subject of decorated papers can be challenging. The vocabulary may be baffling, the methodology intricate, the precise origins difficult to establish. These aspects may inform our appreciation, but no specialist knowledge is needed to appreciate the visual appeal of these amazing objects.

CHRONOLOGY & GEOGRAPHICAL SPREAD

Decorated papers have been produced worldwide for centuries. Traditionally, the invention of paper is attributed to the Chinese court official Cai Lun, who presented his discovery to the Eastern Han emperor in AD 105.[4] According to recent archaeological finds, however, it now seems that a rudimentary form of paper was in existence earlier.[5] Cai Lun, it appears, radically improved its quality and made it more economically viable. Coloured papers were in use from the first century AD, but the circumstances surrounding the emergence of decorated paper remain a mystery.[6] China produced block-printed illustration in the ninth century, and a description of colour-sprinkled paper is included in a Chinese book of 968, *Four Implements for Writing in a Scholar's Studio* by Su-I-chien, but no examples have as yet come to light.[7]

The Japanese adopted block printing later than the Chinese, during the seventeenth century.[8] The earliest datable sample of marbled paper comes from Japan, in the form of a book of 1118 entitled *The Poetical Works of Thirty-six Men*, which contains sheets of *suminagashi* (water marbling). During the Heian period (AD 794–1185), the use of decorated paper for copying sutras was common; by the Muromachi period (1392–1573), it was well established.[9] Decorated paper became a vital component of seventeenth-century luxury editions of literary works, as confirmed by the scholar of Japanese culture Peter Kornicki: 'At their most luxurious they could have patterns printed in colour and crests stamped in gold and silver, as did the paper used by the calligrapher and courtier Karasumaru Mitsuhiro for some poems he copied out in the 1630s.'[10]

Paper-making methods clearly passed along the trade routes, with techniques frequently being adapted to suit local conditions, and it may be that decorating techniques were transferred in a similar fashion.

By the fifteenth century, new methods of production in Europe meant that paper could be produced more easily than parchment. It was cheaper to buy, much more versatile than other mediums and its quality was such that it was even imported by some Near Eastern countries for marbling. Perhaps decoration went some way towards masking inferior paper. As the artist and researcher Rebecca Salter suggests, 'It is possible that the impetus for highly decorated papers was as prosaic as a shortage of materials for paper-making and a need to disguise the rather dull appearance of recycled paper.'[11] An inexpensive paper source meant that the use of decorated papers became economically viable. Some methods of production were more exacting in their requirements than others – marbling, for example, requires a source of pure water – and those regions with the right conditions were able to flourish.

The universal desire for the exotic led other countries to try to manufacture their own versions of marbled

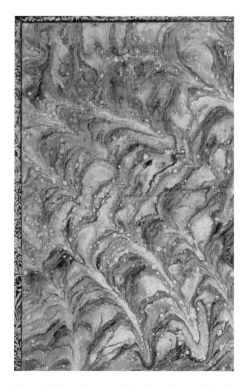

Fig. 1: Eighteenth-century English comb-marbled end-leaves in *The Book of Common Prayer* (John Baskerville: Cambridge, 1760).

paper. The link, if any, between marbling in China or Japan and Central Asia has not been established and differences exist, but the practice spread fairly widely over the Far and Near East. Evidence suggests that marbling was practised in thirteenth-century Turkestan and fourteenth-century Samarkand and Herat, and that it flourished under the Seljuks (the eleventh to twelfth centuries), the Ottomans (from 1299) and the Mughals (sixteenth- to nineteenth-century India). From its Eastern origins it spread westwards, reaching Europe in the seventeenth century, and we know that the French bookbinder Macé Ruette (1584–1644) was renowned for making marbled end-leaves, as were the eighteenth-century Parisian binding families of Derome and Padeloup.[12] In seventeenth-century England, marbled papers were the subject of a lecture by the diarist John Evelyn, while the eighteenth century saw a competition held by the Royal Society of Arts; the printer John Baskerville (1706–1775) was a noted entrant (see fig. 1). The publication in 1853 of *The Art of Marbling* by the bookbinder and marbler Charles Woolnough (*c.* 1812–1880) did much to demystify the craft (to the dismay of many marblers keen to preserve their monopoly).[13]

Block printing on paper was practised in fifteenth-century Europe, notably in Italy (an early source of paper production). As methods improved, workshops began to spring up from the late seventeenth to the early eighteenth century in Paris, Orleans and Tours in France; Augsburg, Nuremberg and Fürth in Germany; and Florence, Venice and Bassano in Italy.

REGIONAL DIFFERENCES

There were clearly national differences regarding the styling and production of pre-industrial European decorated papers. Papers decorated with gold- and silver-coloured designs seem to have been an eighteenth-century German speciality, but other contemporary methods, such as block printing, sprinkling and paste, were more common. In England, marbling seems to have been preferred from the seventeenth century, although, again, other techniques were in use. In contemporary France and Italy, block-printed papers were more popular. Decorated-paper collector Tanya Schmoller notes that the Italian block-printed papers had a 'rough and slightly primitive style

which is very different from the orderly and neatly designed block-printed papers from Northern Europe'.[14] However, it can be difficult to determine the country of origin of certain unsigned block-printed papers. We have seen that paper was widely exported, but craftsmen travelled too, and blocks, plates and stamps were sold and resold, perhaps ending up far from their place of manufacture. Marbling techniques also differ from East to West. Some decoration is made by the combination of techniques, while others mimic one another; Olga Hirsch, for example, categorizes papers J.2747 to J.2752.a as 'lithography imitating paste paper'.[15] Western styles also influenced the East.

Fig. 2: Early American marbled bank note issued by B. F. Bache, the grandson of Benjamin Franklin.

Fig. 3: The Latin phrase (*cum privilegio*) in the border indicates that the paper-decorator Leopold was authorized to make brocade paper. J.97

manufacturers and then exporting them elsewhere. Foreign styles of decorated paper became increasingly popular, and local craftsmen endeavoured to recreate them. We see this in England from the seventeenth century, when efforts were made to produce Persian- and Turkish-style marbling.

National governments adopted policies aimed at raising money from the trade of decorated papers. In eighteenth-century Germany, for example, states granted official licences to publishers and producers of brocade paper (see fig. 3); without such a licence, the work could not be done. The craft supported many families, whose members passed on their skills one to another, and each practitioner jealously guarded his own

In seventeenth- to eighteenth-century China, for instance, the emperors required their own workshops to use patterns from Western gold-decorated papers.[16] All we can be sure of is that date, geographical location, the availability of raw materials and artistic trends are all contributing factors to function, style and technique.

THE IMPACT OF DECORATED PAPERS

In practice, decorated papers were an important resource for governments, although the part they had to play was often obscure and unacknowledged. It is easy to appreciate how the possession of, say, water or precious metals influences a national economy; decorated papers, however, cannot be categorized in the same way. Despite this, such papers are associated with vitally important developments. Early experiments with paper currency (called 'flying cash') in China during the Song and Ming dynasties (AD 960–1279 and 1368–1644 respectively) relied on block-printed paper featuring decorative borders composed of dragons (a motif symbolizing the emperor). According to the statesman and inventor Benjamin Franklin, his introduction of bank notes printed on marbled paper (to counter fraud; see fig. 2) was instrumental in the victory of the United States in the American War of Independence (1775–83).[17]

Decorated papers were traded widely, and the customs duties levied on them provided a steady income for the national purse. The Netherlands in particular benefited from their trade, receiving deliveries from

Fig. 4: Paper from the Réveillon workshop in Paris, *c.* 1745. J.1389

FUSILLADE AU FAUXBOURG S.^T ANTOINE,
Le 28 Avril 1789.

Fig. 5: The Réveillon workshop in Paris under attack in April 1789. From *Collection complète des tableaux historiques de la Révolution française* (1804).

methods while trying to poach the successful techniques of his competitors. Inevitably, corporations were formed to regulate business, one example being the guild of *dominotiers* (makers of decorated paper) formed in Paris in 1586.

Fortunes could certainly be made in the paper-printing trade. One successful business in Bassano was run by the Remondini family. Giuseppe Remondini, recorded as the owner in 1796, was ennobled by the Venetian Republic and lived in a castle.[18] The production of decorated paper was no guarantee of financial success, however, and tradesmen frequently combined this activity with others in an attempt to bolster business. Bookbinders would routinely make their own decorated paper (often of the paste or marbled variety) to save money. The manufacturers of 'fancy' paper, as it was sometimes known in Victorian England, offered as wide a product choice as was possible. Frederick Reni Renvoize, 'Licensed Enamelled Card and Drawing Board Maker, Hot Presser, Paper Glazer, Enamelled Paper Colourer, and General Manufacturing Stationer to the Trade, and Wholesale Fancy Paper Stainer [decorator], Colour and Varnish Maker', owned more than five workshops in east London but was declared bankrupt on 25 March 1854 and imprisoned.[19] Employees were similarly affected. In a trial at the Guildhall in London in August 1869, Mrs Freeman, a widow who had been robbed of her last shilling, 'stated that she worked at the fancy-paper trade but it was so slack just now that last week she only earned 6 shillings and 5 shillings the week before'.[20]

Paper decorators were as susceptible as any other craftsmen to the exigencies of the times in which they lived. In April 1789, at the beginning of the French Revolution, the large paper-printing works owned by Jean-Baptiste Réveillon, 'Manufacture Royale', was attacked by the Paris mob (see figs 4 and 5). Réveillon was not a staunch royalist, but his association with the Ancien Régime made him an obvious target. He fled to England, and his factory (reopened by others) subsequently concentrated on the production of papers in the revolutionary colours of red, white and blue.

There were sound economic and practical reasons for the historical importance of decorated paper, but ideas played their part too, not least those of a spiritual nature. In the Near and Far East in particular, decorated paper could carry artistic or religious significance. This was especially true of marbling, which the Sufi poet Rumi called 'embroidery on water', and of block printing, which was strongly associated with the spread of spiritual ideas in Buddhist China. In Islamic regions, all book arts were highly esteemed because they expressed the word of God, and ornamentation (as opposed to representational imagery) often framed passages from the Koran. One type of marbling demonstrates an explicit link with religion. Known as *hatip ebru* (preacher's marbling), it was named after Mehmet Efendi, an eighteenth-century preacher who practised at an Istanbul mosque, probably Hagia Sophia in modern-day Istanbul. A nineteenth-century style has also been associated with a particular Sufi order, through Şeyh Sadık Efendi (d. 1846) and his sons.[21]

WHAT WERE DECORATED PAPERS USED FOR?

As befits the diverse character of decorated papers, some functions were universal, others regional. They feature widely, for example, as wrappers for books, backing for playing cards and linings for chests and cases. Countries as disparate as China, Britain and the United States relied on them for paper currency. In both East and West, block prints found favour in the humblest of homes, and we should not discount their importance in a harsh environment that lacked the comforts we now take for granted. To the impoverished, the effects of ornamentation were much appreciated. In Christian societies, such as sixteenth-century Germany, holy pictures could be purchased in churches. The religious reformer Martin Luther reported that monasteries were deserted except for a single friar, 'who sits all day in the church to sell souvenirs and little pictures to pilgrims'.[22] During the same period

Fig. 6: Three panels taken from a gold brocade paper attributed to Johann Lechner (c. 1790–1839) of Fürth, Germany. J.317

in Antwerp, it was customary to give children coloured block prints of saints on Shrove Tuesday to ward off evil.[23] In China, many people displayed a printed charm outside their house to protect its inhabitants from fire. Similarly, in Japan, a paper decorated with a swallow would encourage good luck, fidelity in marriage and fertility. The English engraver Thomas Bewick recorded that in the first half of the eighteenth century, popular woodcuts were to be seen 'in every farmhouse, cottage and hovel'.[24] Moreover, ordinary people were able to draw both instruction and comfort from such objects as the block-printed images of saints sold in France by *dominotiers*; the gold-coloured scenes from the Bible created by German paper decorators; and the lively depictions of the alphabet, numerals or exotic animals that could be found on many papers (see figs 6 and 7). The young Goethe prized sheets such as this. He noted that children were prepared to spend more than a penny at the paper-selling stalls to buy colourful sheets decorated with 'animaux dorés'.[25]

At a much more basic level, certain foodstuffs are known to have been wrapped in decorated paper (gingerbread is the example most often cited; see fig. 8), while it was also regularly employed by certain domestic arts: *chiyogami*, a vibrant style of Japanese block-printed paper, was used in origami, as well as for toys and dolls. In China, decorated foil papers known as 'tea chest' papers were produced to replace the poisonous lead linings of the crates used for transporting the commodity. A perusal of Victorian newspapers reveals that decorated papers were used to cover firework cases, medicinal pill boxes ('the boxes in marbled paper and marked "B" are a more active preparation than the others') and 'dainty gold paper cigarette boxes exquisitely embossed in figures' intended for women.[26] Today, artisan chocolate-makers in Brooklyn in the United States and Oporto in Portugal wrap their goods in Italian block-printed papers featuring traditional designs.[27]

Decorated papers had their uses in the homes of the wealthy too, not least the highest in the land. South Asian potentates wrote to their fellow rulers on decorated paper as a mark of status.[28] Indeed, it was the obvious choice for *any* petitioner, since such a document would be sure to catch the eye. We know that an Italian abbot sent Queen Elizabeth I of England a letter 'on a very particular Paper, adorn'd all about the Border with Emblems & Mottos in Gold; & the back all decorated with golden Darts'.[29]

Decorated papers served a very practical function in the richer households. They were used to cover the

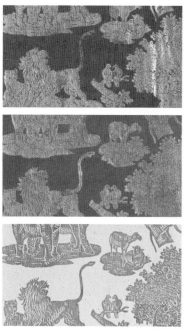

Fig. 7: Differently coloured examples of an eighteenth-century brocade paper by G. N. & Abel Renner of Nuremberg. J.295, J.297, J.296

Fig. 8: Wrapping paper for foodstuffs, Germany, *c.* 1860–70. J.1156

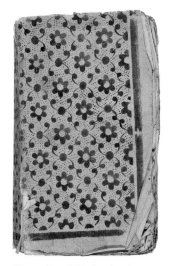

Fig. 9: Detail of *The Music Lesson* (c. 1662–5) by Vermeer, showing the use of decorated papers on a virginal.

Fig. 10: French block-printed paper cover on an issue of the poetry journal *Almanach des muses* from 1782. B.105

Fig. 11: Comb-marbled end-leaf from John Evelyn's gold-tooled leather prayer book, a present from his sister Elizabeth in 1685. Eve.22.a.1–3

rough edges and interiors of such manufactured goods as embroidered vanity cases, cupboards and desks (including the drawers, pigeon holes and any secret compartments). They were also utilized to decorate parts of musical instruments, such as the keywell of a virginal or the lid of a harpsichord (see fig. 9). As the eighteenth century progressed, paper began to replace tapestries and textiles on the walls of the palaces of royalty and aristocracy. (In fact, woodblock-printed wallpaper was being exported from France by the 1680s, with the Papillon family of wood engravers serving as the pioneers of the Paris trade. Wallpaper as a craft came into its own with the invention of rolls of paper and associated machinery.) Réveillon papers became a popular export to the United States during the 1700s, and can still be seen in certain New England homes.

Some types of decorated paper were restricted to the upper ranks of society, and not just because they were expensive to buy. Use of *suminagashi* in Japan was confined to the imperial court until 1585, after which time its use was extended to the display of handwritten poetry, decorative screens in houses and linings for boxes. Wealthy students travelling in Europe in the seventeenth and eighteenth centuries sometimes treated themselves to an expensively bound autograph book (*album amicorum*, or *Stammbuch* in German) containing a variety of decorated papers (commonly silhouette, stencil and marbled), which they encouraged their fellow students to sign.

Sheets with marbled backgrounds (sometimes stencilled) and marbled edges were used for official documents, since the complexity of the decoration made forgery difficult. The techniques were kept secret and handed down covertly from master to apprentice. This practice inevitably led to a monopoly: in Japan, the Hiroba family controlled all *suminagashi* production from 1151 (when a god reputedly gave them the 'recipe') until the end of the sixteenth century. The business proved lucrative, for the family's products continued to be in great demand not only for official but also for cultural purposes, with professional and amateur calligraphers in particular finding that such paper was perfect for the display of poetic verses. Marbled paper inspired a particular reverence when used to display passages copied from the Koran. It does not seem to have had a similar resonance in Western Europe.

Decorated papers have a strong association with the literary world. Papers were (and still are) used as both permanent and temporary book covers, end-leaves and slipcases (see figs 10, 11 and 13). The library of the diarist Samuel Pepys (1633–1703), a noted collector of bookbindings, included wrappers made from decorated paper. Among them were some bronze varnish papers of the type first made in Augsburg between 1692 and 1695, making Pepys an early owner of this new style.[30]

Pepys's fellow diarist John Evelyn carried out research on marbled papers, and in 1661 presented a scholarly paper on the subject to the Royal Society.[31] Albums of calligraphy or painted miniatures frequently featured marbled, stencilled and silhouette papers (see fig. 12), while in eighteenth-century Europe, gold-coloured paper was often used to cover books intended to be given as presents, since it made the binding look more expensive.

Stationers used different styles of paper for invitations, writing paper, cards and wrapping paper. Today, decorated papers are used extensively by the makers of scrapbooks, greetings cards and journals; indeed, some of them produce their own papers. Designs can be downloaded from the Internet, and computer programs simulating the effects of marbling on paper have been developed.

It is no coincidence that the terms used to describe decorated papers, such as 'brocade' and 'cotton', often invoke those of the textile industry. In eighteenth-century Germany, France and Italy – the origin of several types of decorated paper – the printing processes would have had much in common, although there is no firm evidence to suggest that the same block was used on both paper and cloth.[32] Some papers resembled fabric in their tactile qualities, featuring designs cut in positive and negative relief, or crinkled in the manner of crêpe. Batik techniques were also applied to paper and cloth, while flock-covered papers (in German, *velours*) were raised from the surface like suede. In Japan, *katagami* refers to that country's tradition of cutting designs into waterproof paper to use as stencils in the printing of fabrics (see fig. 14). Motifs popular in *chiyogami* were frequently inspired by patterned silk kimonos.

The connections between the decorated-paper and textile industries also extended to storage and packing. The boxes in which nineteenth-century American gentlemen stored their detachable shirt collars ('band boxes') were covered in decorated paper manufactured in the United States itself.[33]

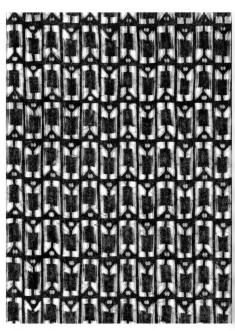

Fig. 12: Marbled-paper border surrounding watercolour in seventeenth-century Indian album. Or. Ms. 2839

Fig. 13: Paste-paper slipcase made for a German hymn book from the 1790s. B.16

Fig. 14: Nineteenth- to early twentieth-century Japanese *katagami* stencil. J.3561

*Eric Ravilious
Lithography from
Wood-engraving*

Fig. 15: Twentieth-century lithograph by Eric Ravilious. J.2881

DECORATED PAPERS IN ART

Historic decorated papers may be regarded as works of art, since a measure of artistry was involved in their production. Inevitably, however, opinions on this matter vary. Some contemporary commentators, including Erasmus (1466–1536), regarded black-and-white block prints, such as those by Albrecht Dürer (1471–1528), as superior to those that had been subsequently coloured by hand.[34] This judgment cannot have been very influential: the market for coloured prints continued to flourish. The Mack family ran a particularly successful colouring business in sixteenth-century Nuremberg.[35] All block prints required visual appeal to be commercially viable, whether the customer was a connoisseur or a tradesman. The art historian Susan Dackerman emphasizes that it is important to situate decorated papers 'within a broader material culture, examining their function and [the] context in which they were produced and used'.[36]

In her book on paste papers, the paper-decorator Susanne Krause urges us to 'forget about art when making decorated paper. Art is something that is unique and neither intended nor suitable for repetition. Decorated paper is repetition, is intended for further processing, is in probably 99 cases out of 100 intended to be cut up and part of something else.'[37] I would favour a broader view. Decorated papers call for imagination in their design and for skill in their production; and even after mechanical reproduction became common in the craft, a certain degree of inspiration and artistic judgment was still required. Indeed, many established artists of the twentieth century, famed for precisely such gifts, were employed in the production of decorated papers (see below).

Unfortunately, the identities of many of the historic craftsmen remain unknown, but this may eventually be resolved by further research (although secrecy was necessary to guard valuable techniques). Manuscripts sometimes reveal details of practitioners. The title of Fuzuli's 'Hadikat-us sueda' (Garden of Happiness), for example, is followed by the phrase 'Ma Sebek Mehmet Ebrisi' (with *ebru* of Sebek Mehmet), 'ebru' being the Turkish term for marbling.[38] The owners of eighteenth-century French, Italian and German workshops

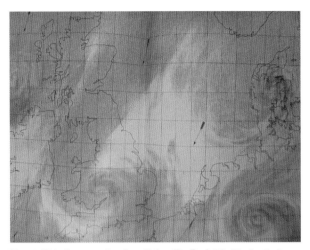

Fig. 16: This diagram, taken from Robert FitzRoy's *The Weather Book* (London, 1863), illustrates the meeting of polar and tropical currents but also resembles a marbled pattern.

Fig. 17: Twentieth-century English marbling, described as a 'doodle' by Sydney (Sandy) Cockerell (1906–1987), the owner of a celebrated marbling workshop in Grantchester, Cambridgeshire. J.2160.h

frequently signed their names in the borders of their block-printed and brocade papers. One eighteenth-century maker, Jean-Michel Papillon, who had learned wood engraving and paper decoration in his father's Paris workshop, received recognition for his artistry when he was elected to the Société des Arts in 1773 (although this was probably due more to his skill as an engraver than to his talents as a paper decorator).

Mass production inevitably altered the nature of the craftsman's artistic input, while it became quicker and easier to incorporate new artistic trends. Such techniques as lithography allowed a number of artists, including Edward Bawden, Paul Nash, Graham Sutherland and Eric Ravilious (see fig. 15), to produce paper designs, notably in England at the Curwen Press from the 1920s. Furthermore, automated processes were devised that enabled marbled patterns to be produced in quantities. Today, decorated papers celebrate the skills of graphic designers and other book artists. An exciting example of such work is that of Tini Miura, who has made decorated papers for wrapping and boxes used by a popular Japanese shop.[39]

A pattern can bring pleasure to both rich and poor, to both the educated and the illiterate, and this can be enough. A well-constructed design, however, also has the power to intrigue. Patterns can convey information directly, as in a diagram (see fig. 16), or they can have a subliminal effect, altering the way in which we view the world.

In the words of the philosopher Isaiah Berlin, 'To understand is to perceive patterns.'[40] Indeed, the ability to distinguish differences and similarities is an important part of the learning process, both for the human brain and for artificial intelligence. The differences between decorated papers carry the analogy further: block printing is repetitive, and there is less room for error or sudden inspiration; in marbling, the swirl of paint transferred to a sheet of paper can be unpredictable for novices (although less so for the experienced practitioner). Designs can provide a focus for meditation, or can be fashioned into recognizable shapes, bringing order to chaos (see fig. 17). The fractal studies of Benoit Mandelbrot and others in the 1970s show that even the most evolving matter (clouds, for example) or images (as in marbling) contain order at a basic level.[41]

In some cultures, the meaning behind the artistic depiction of certain objects is widely understood. In

China, for example, peonies are associated with wealth, and chrysanthemums with long life. Japanese crafts also use motifs for communication, some inspired by the Shinto religion or Buddhism: bamboo represents strength of character, the koi carp worldly aspiration and achievement, tenacity and bravery. The meaning would be comprehended by all.

CONCLUSION

An informed onlooker could appreciate an individual decorated paper as he or she might appreciate a painting. They would have the ability to make reasonable deductions as to where, when and how it was made, and even (to an extent) as to the status of the original purchaser. Symbols would be understood. Even the contemporary artistic influences of the practitioner might be evident. Yet this is not the whole story. Unlike expensive oil paintings, decorated papers were available to all but the poorest in society. There was also a huge variety of styles. The choices made in the acquisition of a particular decorated paper can provide us with an insight into the life and character of its purchaser, of someone like us who existed in a very different world. The selection of a colourful sixteenth-century French block-printed image of a saint, for example, might indicate that the purchaser was devout, or at least wanted to appear so; the choice of an eighteenth-century German sheet of alphabets, by contrast, may reveal an individual's educational aspirations or an adventurous spirit. We are also able to see through the eyes of our ancestors. One paper, for instance, shows how a crocodile was perceived in eighteenth-century Germany (see fig. 18).

It can require imagination to understand just how visually exciting these papers were. Some have faded over time, or are covered in gold that has turned green (owing to the presence of copper in the alloy) or silver that has blackened (owing to oxidization; see fig. 19).

Decorated papers offer much more than a mere backdrop to the era in which they were created. There is still scope for discovery. Why did the English enthusiastically adopt marbled papers when the Scots preferred gold? Why, for that matter, did European marbling develop in such a different way from the Turkish styles on which it was based? Fashion, access to materials (the astragalus plant, whose resin makes the water more viscous in Turkish marbling, is absent in Europe) and different cultural imperatives must all be considered. In 1878 Charles Woolnough delivered a lecture on marbling to the Royal Society of Arts entitled 'A Pretty Mysterious Art'.[42] Since then, we have learned a great deal more about decorated papers, but elements of this mystery remain to intrigue us.

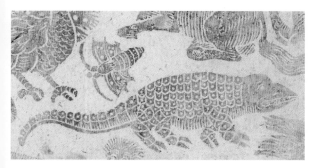

Fig. 18: Detail from eighteenth-century German brocade paper showing a crocodile. J.300

Fig. 19: Eighteenth-century German brocade paper with silver-coloured relief that has oxidized. J.40

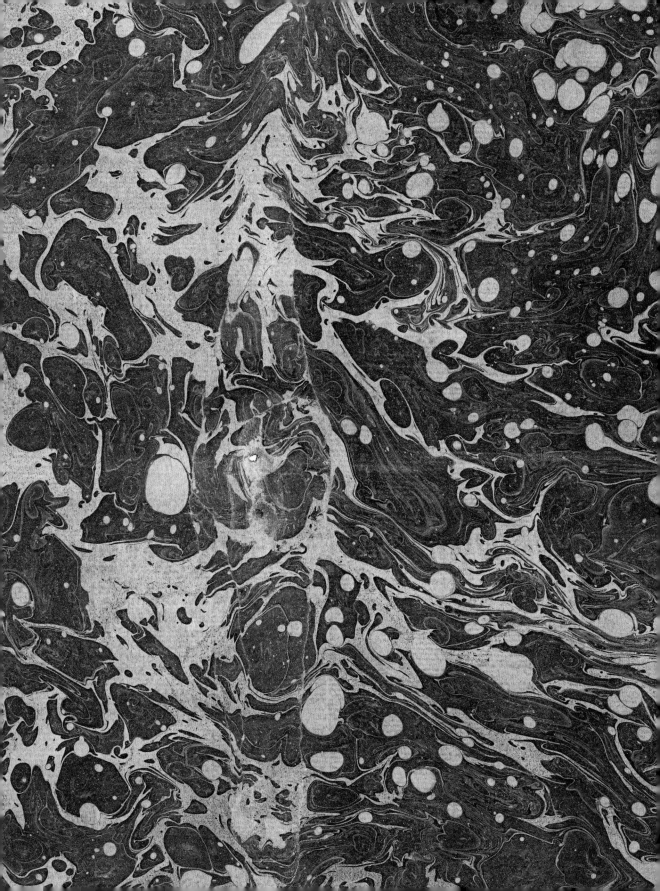

HAND-MARBLED PAPERS

Fig. 1: Twentieth-century British *suminagashi* by Victoria Hall. Add.15

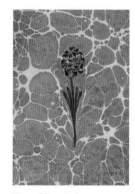

Fig. 2: Twentieth-century marbled paper by Necmettin Okyay. J.3526.a.(v)

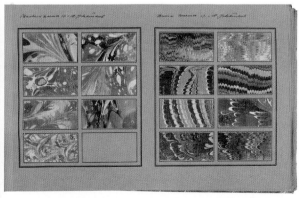

Fig. 3: Page from Olga Hirsch's scrapbook featuring different styles of marbled papers. Ref. 16

Marbling is a process easier described than achieved. Requirements for marbling are few: a tray for the marbling base, inks or paints, and pattern-making tools (e.g. a straw, a fan, horsehair, a comb or a stylus). In the Japanese tradition of *suminagashi*, the marbling base is pure water. Colours are applied to the surface of the water with a fine brush or hair; a dispersant, such as pine oil or perspiration, is also added. Rings take shape, and are manipulated using various tools (see fig. 1). 'Turkish' marbling requires a 'size' (water made viscous with an additive), on to which colours are flicked from a brush or dropped from a pipette and, if desired, manipulated with suitable tools. In both methods, a sheet of paper is carefully placed over the floating pattern in order to capture what is a unique work of art.[1]

In the Near East, notably fifteenth- to sixteenth-century Ottoman Turkey and seventeenth-century Mughal India, royalty and the nobility patronized workshops that produced manuscript copies of the Koran. The flaps of the leather covers in which they were traditionally bound were frequently lined with decorated, often marbled paper. Marbled borders also lent an extra degree of distinction to calligraphy, particularly religious passages copied as an act of devotion. Albums containing paintings and verses in manuscript, often used as a focus for meditation, were also bound using decorated paper. Compiling such collections was a favourite pastime of the Mughal emperor Shah Jahan (1594–1666) and his court.

Abb. 38: Marmorierapparat für zwei Farben (Oskar Sperling, Leipzig)

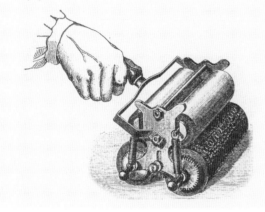

Fig. 4: Nineteenth-century German advertisement showing how two colours might be applied simultaneously via engraved and felt-covered rollers.[10]

Fig. 5: Marbled paper by Paul Kersten, 1899, made at Buntpapierfabrik AG in Aschaffenburg, Germany. J.1808

Innovation prevented marbling from growing moribund. In eighteenth-century Istanbul, Hatip Mehmed Efendi developed a new style based on the manipulation of concentric circles of colour. It was advanced further in the twentieth century by Necmettin Okyay (who refined the art of marbling flowers; see fig. 2), his sons, and his nephew, Mustafa Düzgünman.[2]

Europeans concentrated on mastering the technique for various purposes, and not exclusively to supply the bookbinding trade.[3] The serial counterfeiter William Chaloner easily reproduced the new marbled bank notes issued by the Bank of England in 1695, although a counterfeit was soon traced to his printing press.[4] In 1759 the Society for the Encouragement of Arts, Manufactures and Commerce in London offered an award of £10. 10s. for 'marbling the greatest Quantity of Paper, equal in Goodness to the best marbled Paper imported from abroad, not less than one Rheam [sic]'.[5]

Particular European styles began to emerge (see fig. 3). As the bookbinding historian Mirjam Foot has

noted, however, 'The nomenclature of the various kinds of marbles in different languages is confusing to say the least.'[6] The terms used to describe the different styles include 'Dutch', 'stone', 'curl', 'veined', 'shell', 'comb', 'snail', 'Stormont', 'sunspot', 'peacock', 'bouquet', 'nonpareil' and 'Spanish'.[7] Josef Halfer, a nineteenth-century bookbinder based in Budapest, applied scientific methods to the procedure. The published results transformed the craft. Halfer recommended that carrageenan (a substance extracted from seaweed) be added to the size, thereby extending its lifespan,[8] and his research inspired many innovative patterns in Europe. The German paper-decorating factories also embraced innovation (see figs 4 and 5).

Hand-marbling continues to be popular, although there are very few full-time professionals. It often inspires a thoughtful quality in its practitioners. The inventor Michael Faraday (who trained as a bookbinder) appreciated the craft 'because of the very beautiful principles of natural philosophy which it involves'.[9]

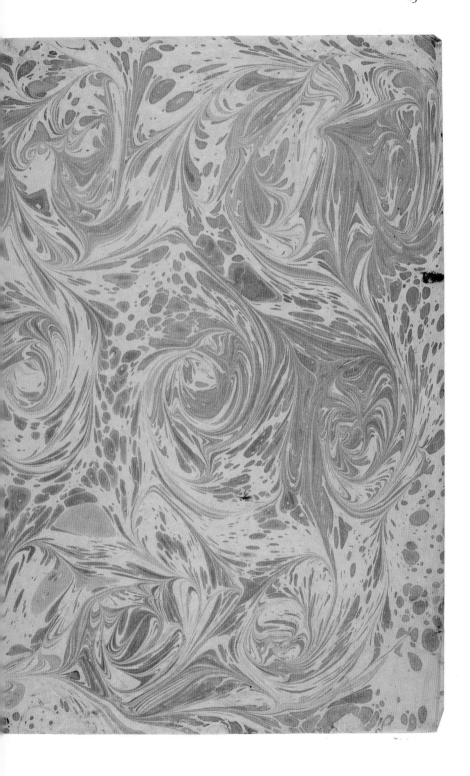

Twentieth century, probably Turkish. The current tradition of marbling in Turkey dates to the middle of the nineteenth century, when the craft was revitalized owing to its adoption by a Sufi order, the demands of the publishing industry and other initiatives. J.3523

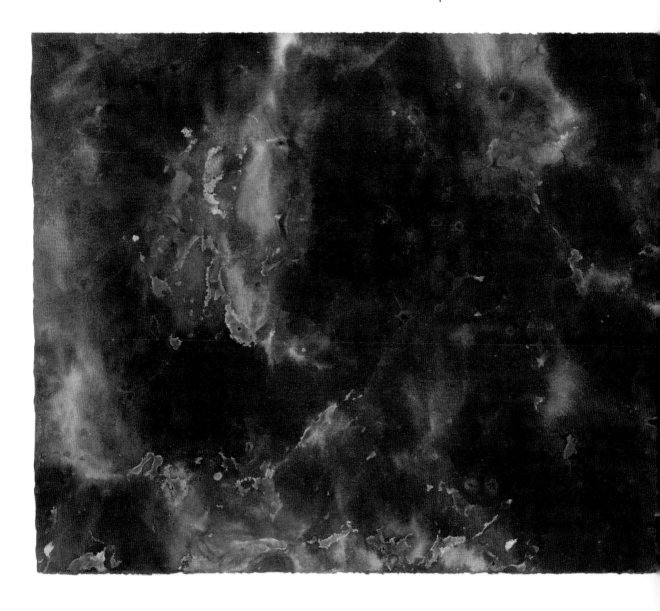

Above and opposite
It may seem perverse to include
these papers here because they
cannot technically be referred to as
examples of marbling; in fact, they
demonstrate clearly what marbling
is not. The paints have mixed
together on the surface of the paper,
whereas marbled paint does not
blend thanks to such preparations
as ox gall, which keep the colours
separate. This method is sometimes
called 'bench marbling' or 'Morris
marbling', after the practitioner
E. W. Morris. J.1994.c, J.1994.d

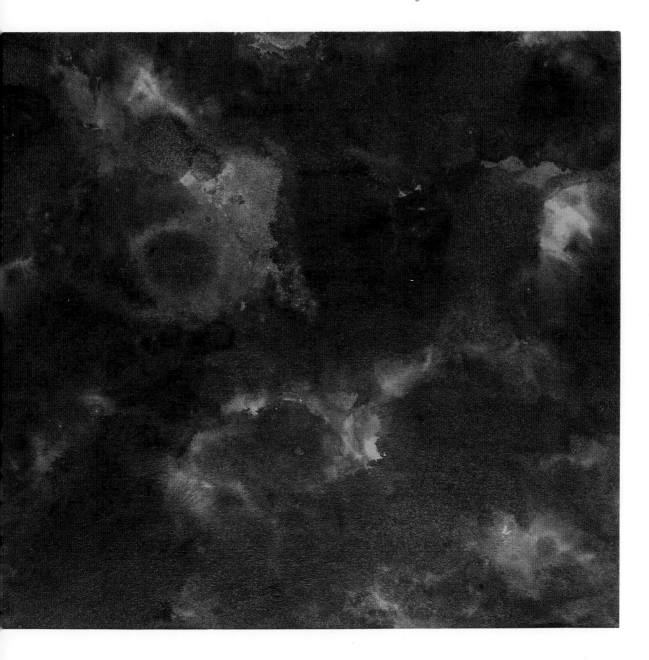

Page 26
Nineteenth-century European
marbling. This basic style is
extremely versatile as it allows the
paints to spread freely. A stylus has
been used subsequently to make the
stone pattern more elaborate. J.1612

Page 27
Probably twentieth-century
Turkish marbling in a common
style similar to European stone
marbling (known as *battal ebru* in
Turkish), but with an added level
of detail using black paint. J.3525

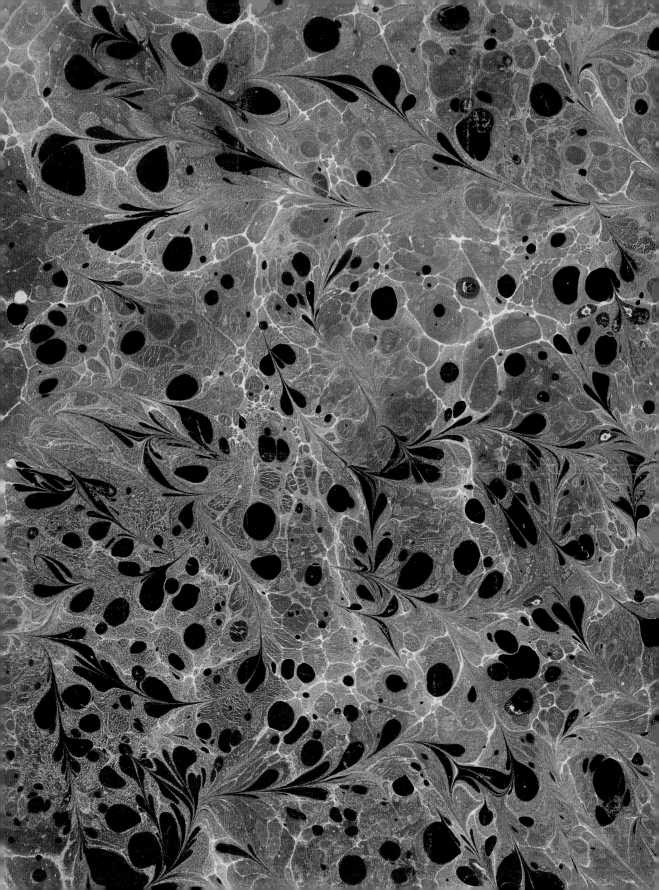

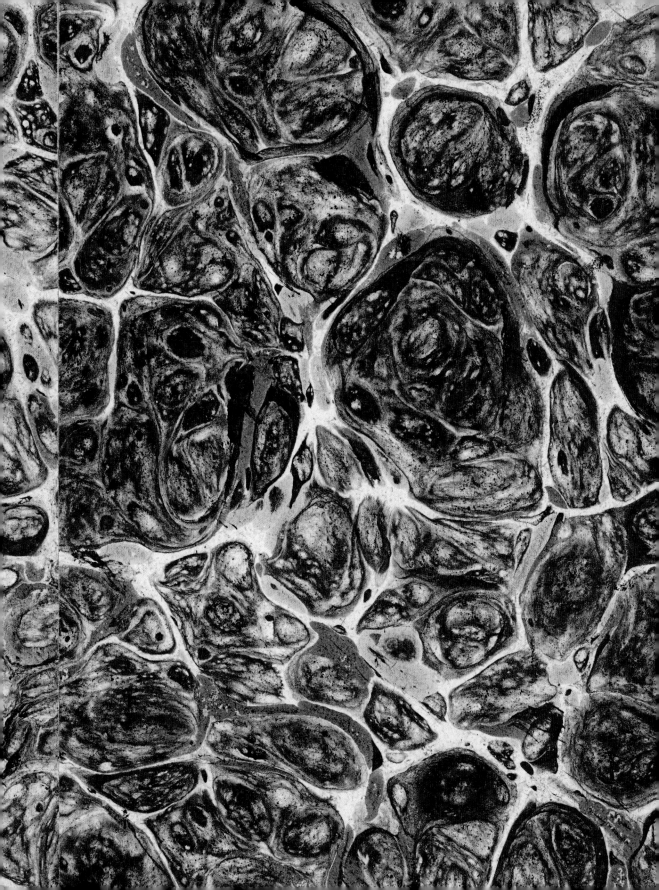

Page 28
Eighteenth-century European
comb marbling. Here, the floating
paints were manipulated using
a rake. Each marbler had his own
favoured methods, although historic
manuals recommended having
a selection of appropriate tools.
J.1625

Page 29
Nineteenth-century European shell
marbling, produced by the addition
of a dispersant (often turpentine).
This style was commonly used for
end-leaves. J.1967

Right
Eighteenth-century European
marbling, a traditional style often
used for end-leaves. According
to Olga Hirsch, the colours seen
here are the same as those referred
to by Diderot and d'Alembert in
their description of marbling in the
*Encyclopédie, ou dictionnaire raisonné
des sciences, des arts et des métiers*
(1751–72). J.1492

Left
Twentieth-century Danish
marbling in oils (*c.* 1961). There
is no evidence of early marbling
in Denmark, although it was
probably imported at the beginning
of the eighteenth century. After
1892, the Copenhagen-based
author and researcher Anker
Kyster popularized the practice
of hand-marbling. Compare this
pattern with those on pages 26
and 33. J.1994.e

Page 32
Twentieth-century European
marbling in oils. The addition
of a dispersant has resulted in
this 'broken' pattern. J.1993

Page 33
Twentieth-century European
marbling. The shades used here
would have been unfamiliar to a
pre-nineteenth-century decorator
such as the British marbler Charles
Woolnough. He recommended
the use of three traditional types of
pigment: 'earth' (naturally occurring
minerals), 'mineral' (a combination
of naturally occurring elements)
and 'lake' (derived from soluble
dye and mineral salt). However,
the nineteenth century saw a
proliferation of newly developed
synthetic colours. J.1994.f

Pages 34–5
Nineteenth-century European
moiré marbling. Ripples have been
introduced to a basic stone-marbled
ground by rocking the sheet of
paper backwards and forwards as it
is placed into the marbling trough,
or by moving the trough itself.
J.1629

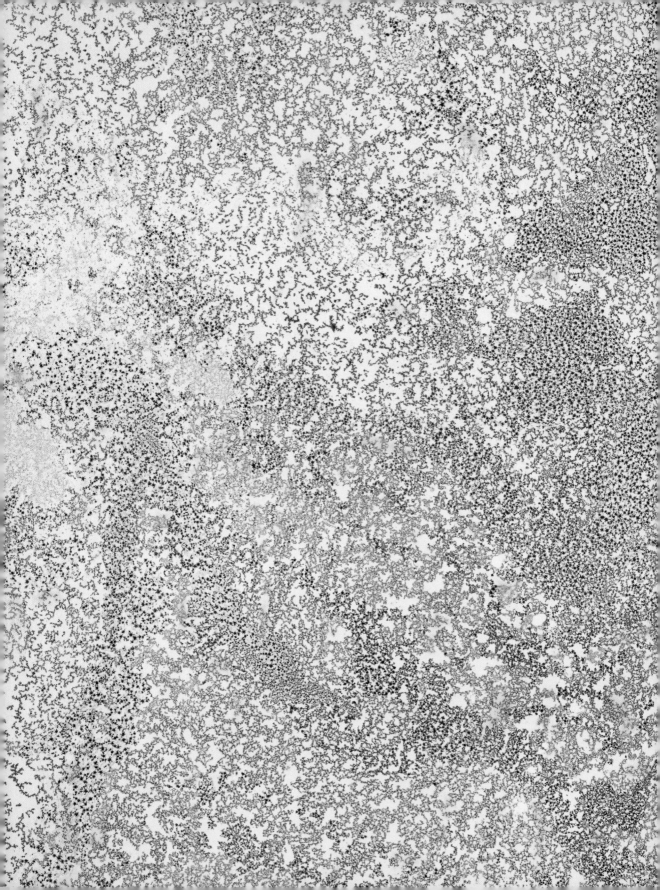

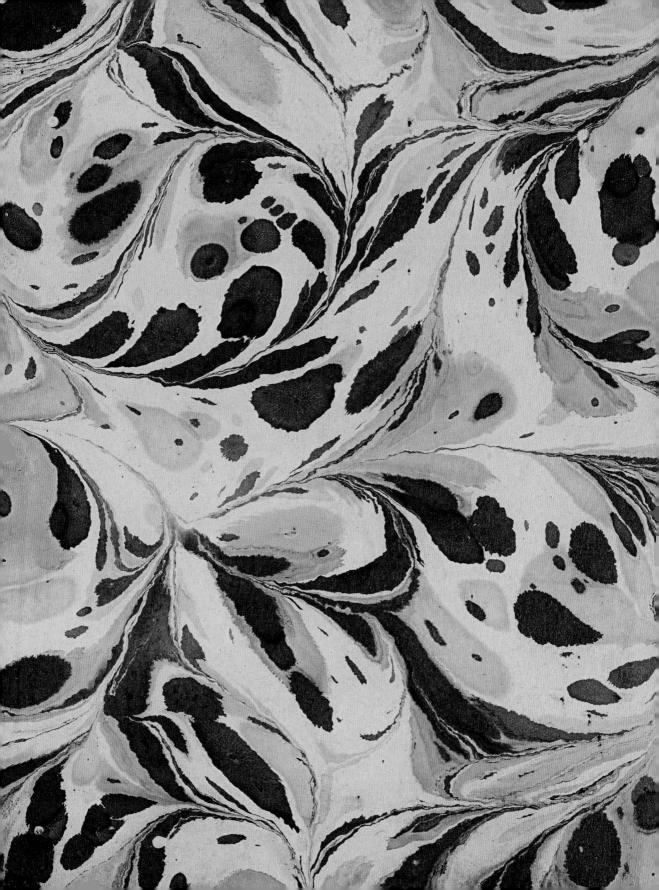

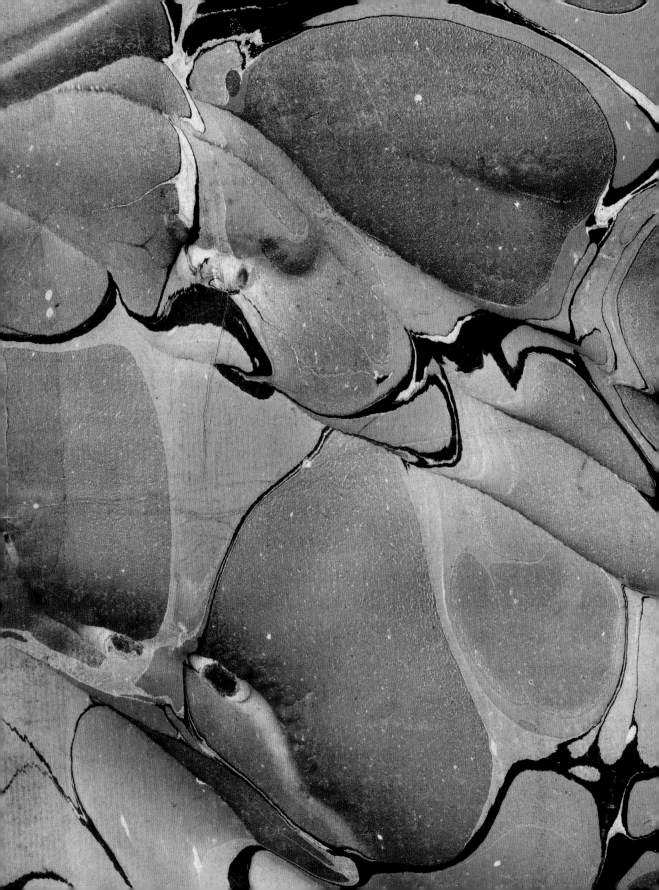

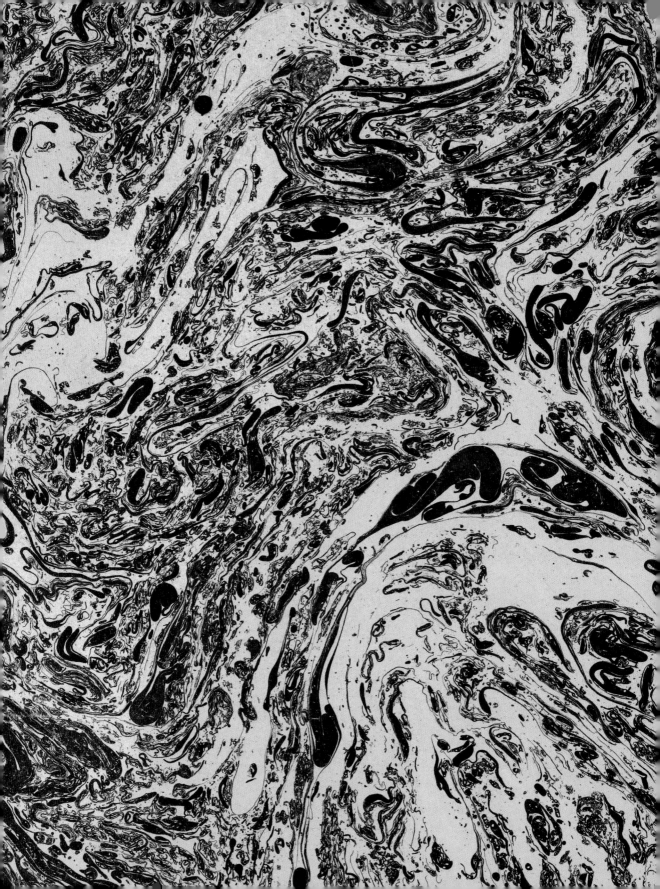

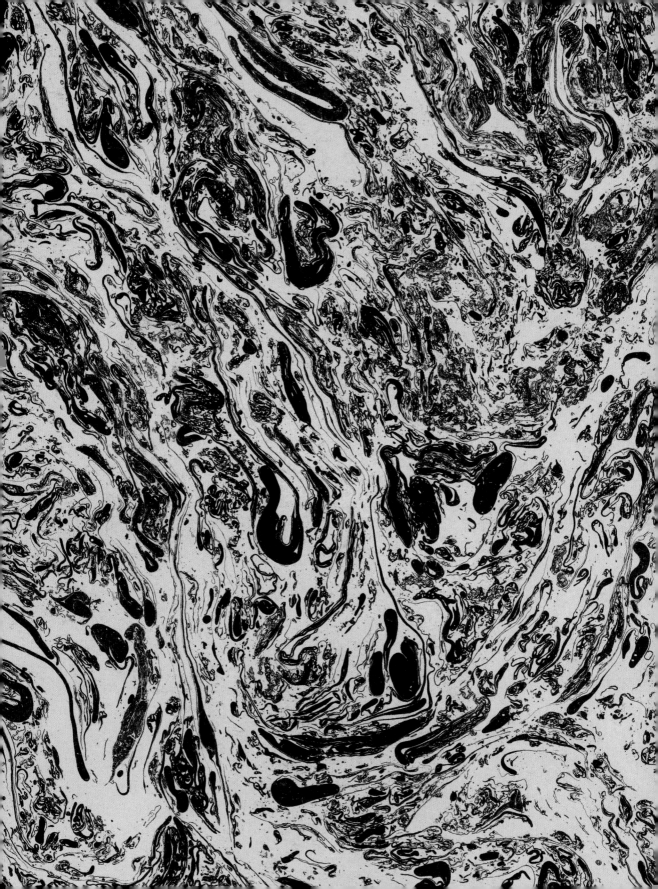

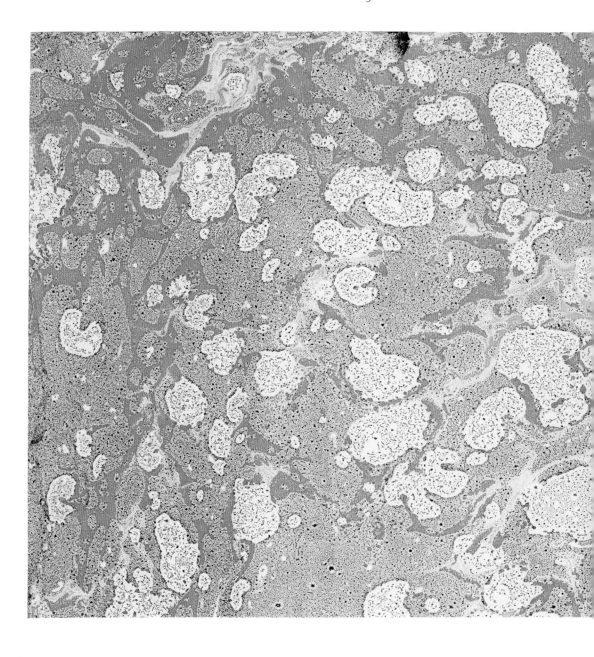

Above and opposite
Twentieth-century European marbling. Superficially, these two examples have much in common, notably the widely sprinkled grey spots and a single dominant colour. On closer inspection, however, it becomes clear that the grey markings in the example above are finer than those in the example opposite, which are larger and more clearly defined. It seems likely that a variety of dispersants were used, but without the marbler's recipe it would be difficult to recreate the patterns. Traditionally, an array of tiny spots with black centres – a style developed in eighteenth-century Germany – was known as 'lead shot', or *Schrot* in German. J.1994.g, J.1994.h

Pages 36–7
Twentieth-century German marbling by the bookbinder and writer Dorothea Freise (1895–1962). J.1989

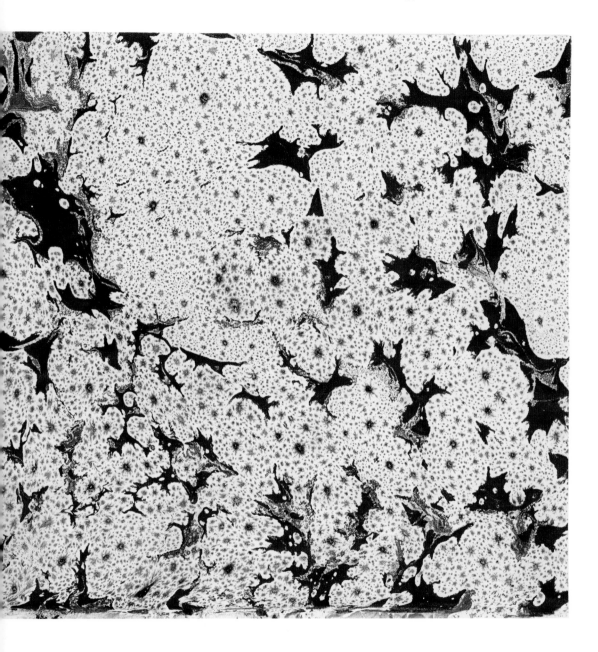

Page 40
Nineteenth-century British
marbling (*c.* 1850), commonly
used for end-leaves. J.1688.a

Page 41
Early twentieth-century English
comb marbling with a curl by
G. W. Gwynne & Sons for the
Doves Press, London. Marbling
was not a lucrative trade, so
Gwynne combined it with edge
decoration. The edges of text blocks
could be marbled, stained or gilt.
J.2001

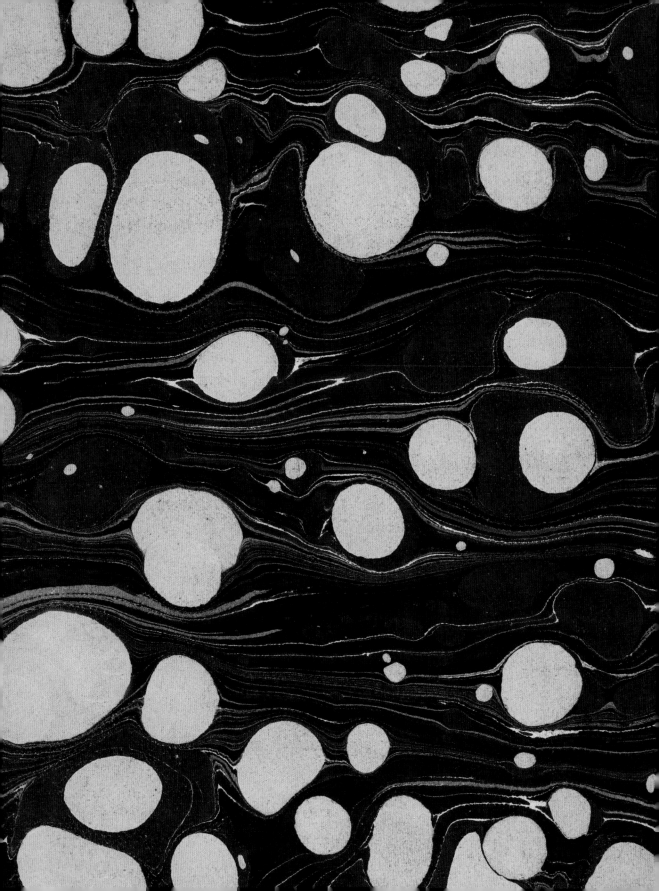

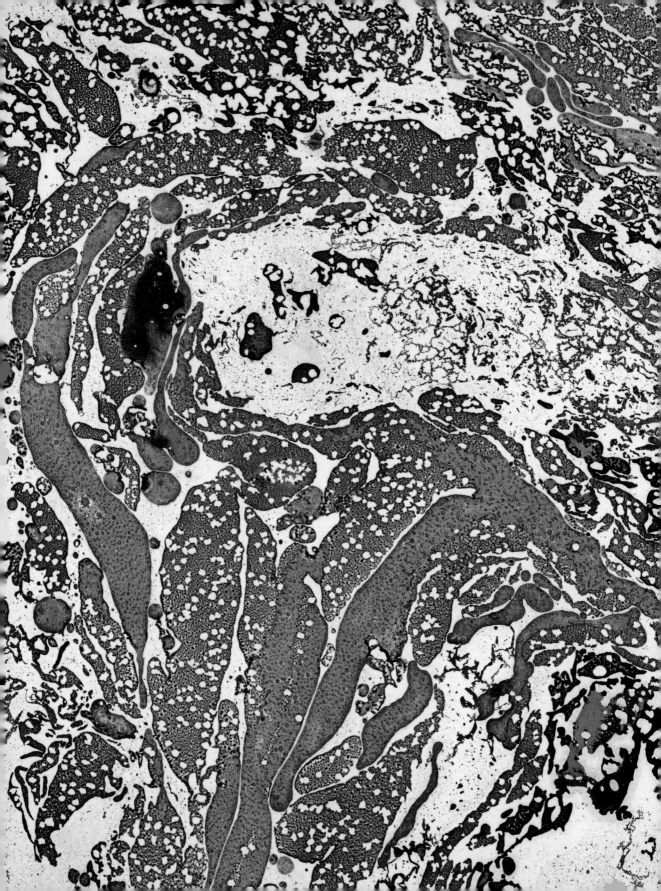

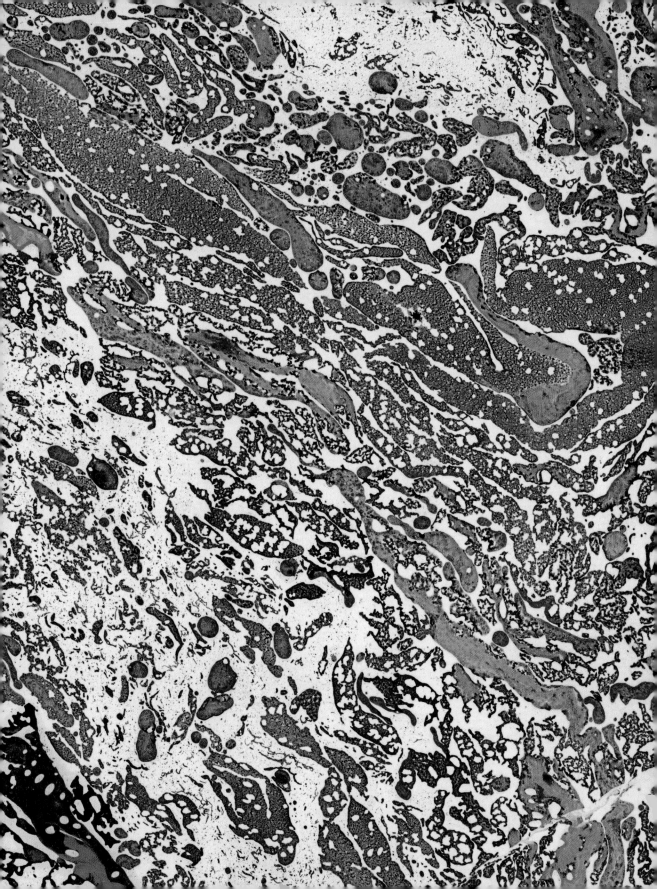

Pages 42–3
Twentieth-century German
marbling in oils by Paul Kersten
(1865–1943). Kersten published
Die Marmorierkunst in 1922
after absorbing both the
traditional techniques of his
bookbinder father and grandfather
and improvements made in the
nineteenth century by Josef Halfer
and his pupil Josef Hauptmann.
J.2025

Right
Eighteenth-century European
comb marbling featuring
the 'traditional' colour palette
of seventeenth- and eighteenth-
century British and French
marblers. J.1636

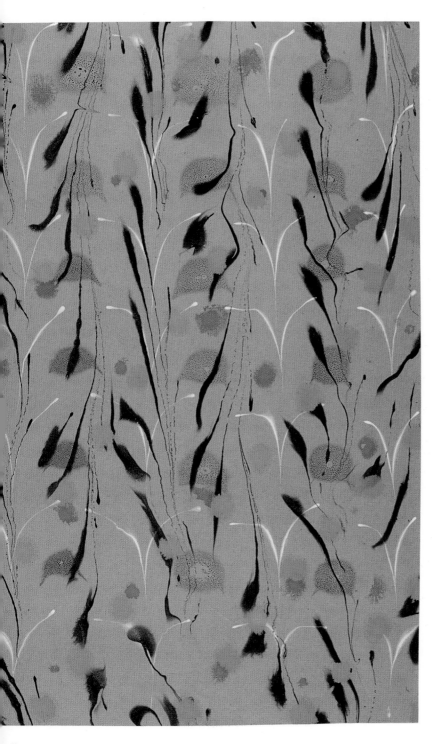

Above
Tirzah Ravilious (1908–1951), whose work from 1938 is shown here, was one of many twentieth-century European women artists who experimented with new directions in marbling. J.2021

Page 46
Twentieth-century European marbling. It seems likely that the 'gritty' appearance seen here has been achieved using a dispersant. The effect is particularly tactile, in contrast to earlier traditional marbles, which can appear smooth. J.2033

Page 47
Twentieth-century European comb marbling. The juxtaposition of paints is the key to marbling, but the selection of colours is also crucial. The bold yellow seen here has been manipulated in such a way as to add life and movement to the surface of the paper. J.2034

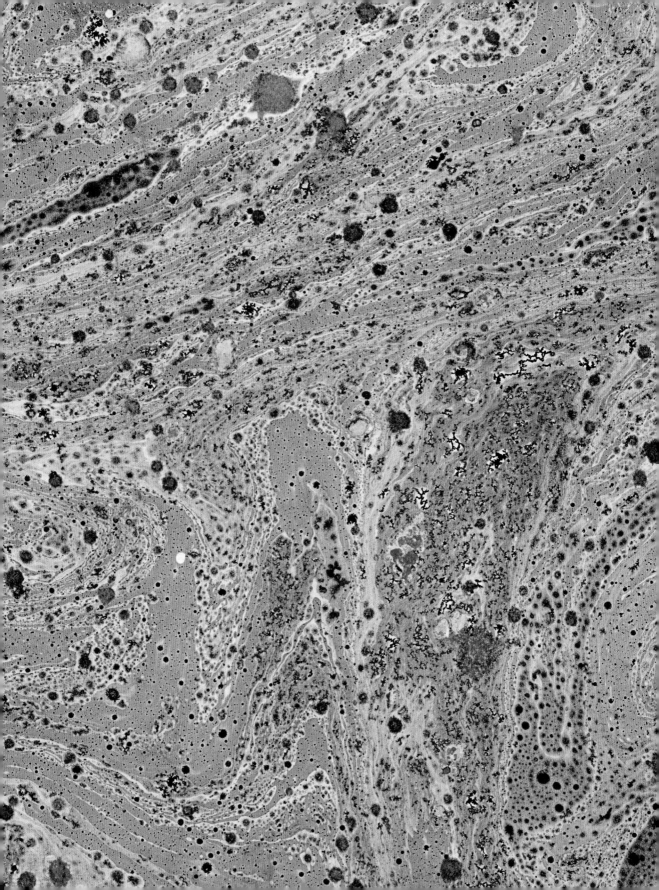

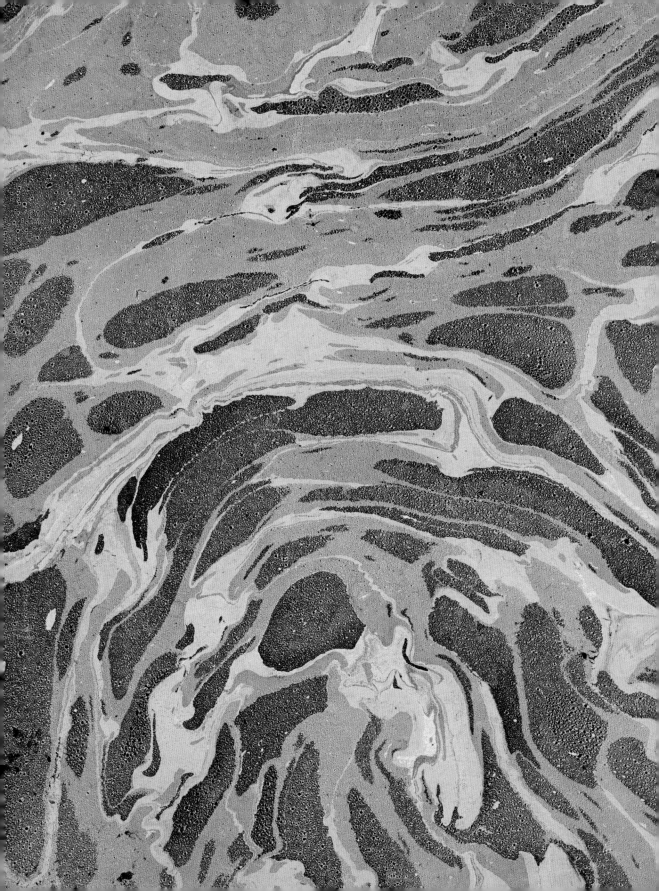

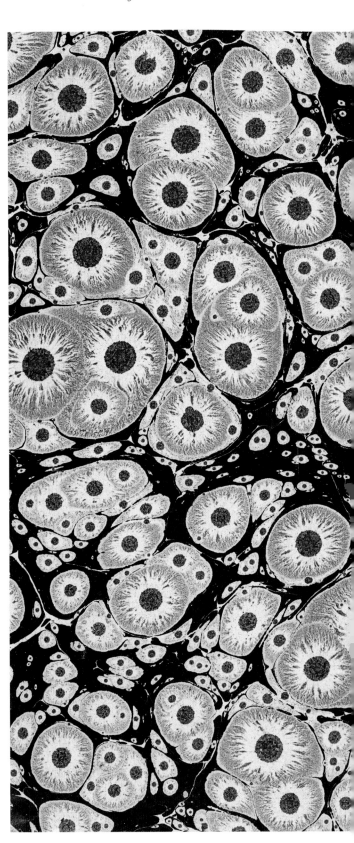

Page 48
Late nineteenth-century German marbling in oils by Paul Kersten (1898), combining conventional and twentieth-century techniques. At first glance this seems a traditional marble, but closer examination reveals the tiny grey dots, probably achieved via the use of a dispersant. J.2024

Page 49
Twentieth-century English comb marbling by Cockerell & Son. The bookbinder Sandy Cockerell believed that it was possible to teach marbling at all levels. His instructional pamphlet, *Marbling Paper as a School Subject*, was published in 1934. His work for professionals, *Marbled Papers* (1966), was described by Mirjam Foot as 'a model of clarity'. J.2049

Right
Nineteenth- to twentieth-century European sunspot, or 'tiger eye', marbling. In the 1850s new chemicals began to be added to the marbling recipes. Caustic substances were particularly effective. Here, a dissolving medium, such as creolin, created the halos around the 'nuclei'; these halos then radiated outwards into the grey. J.1973

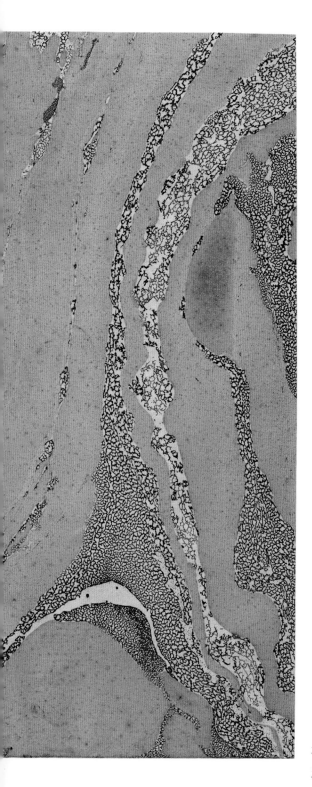

Left
Twentieth-century German
marbling in oils by Paul Kersten.
This pattern shows Kersten as an
innovator in his use of colours and
abstract motifs, which at the time
were uncommon on end-leaves.
J.2027

Pages 52–3
Eighteenth-century European
snail marbling, also known as
'French curl'. This was a traditional
style used for the end-leaves in
French and British books of
the seventeenth century. In his
Art of Marbling (London, 1853),
Charles Woolnough recommended
procuring 'a frame with as many
pegs as you require curls on your
sheet'. J.1769

Pages 54–5
Twentieth-century Turkish
marbling. This pattern
demonstrates how the newly added
paints push aside the previously
applied ones. A dispersant causes
the formation of the white spots,
the size of which is determined
by the quantity of dispersant used.
J.3526.a.1

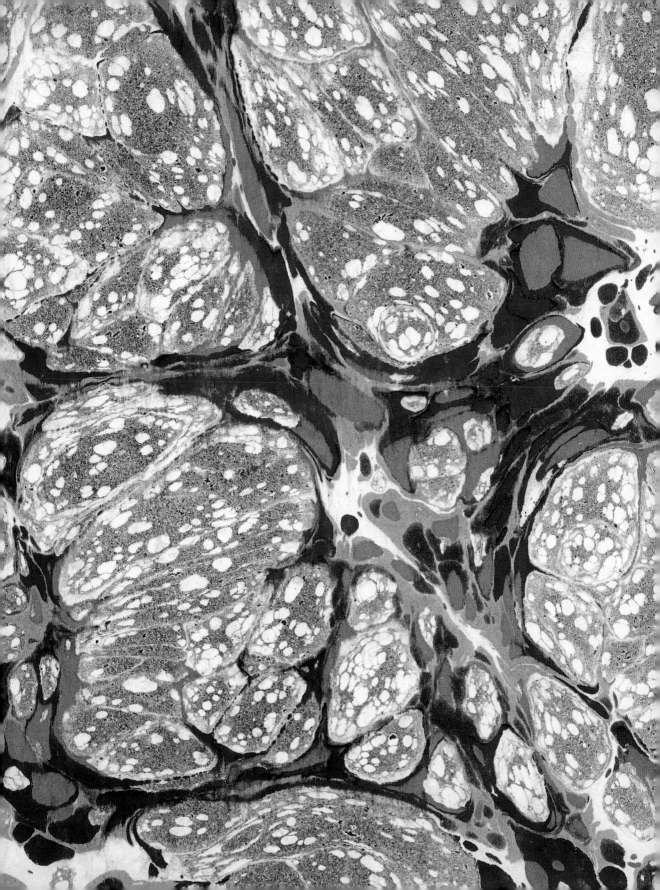

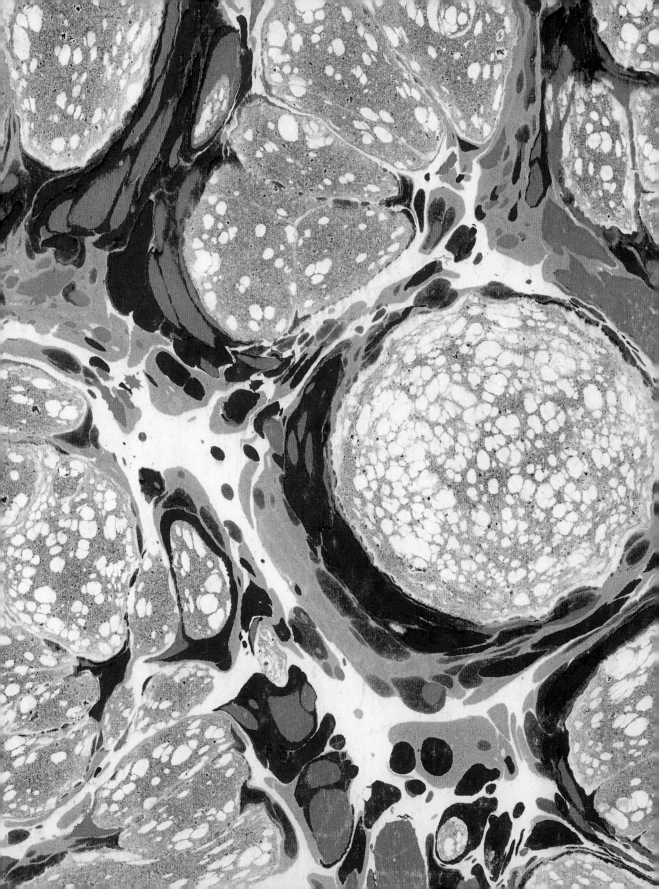

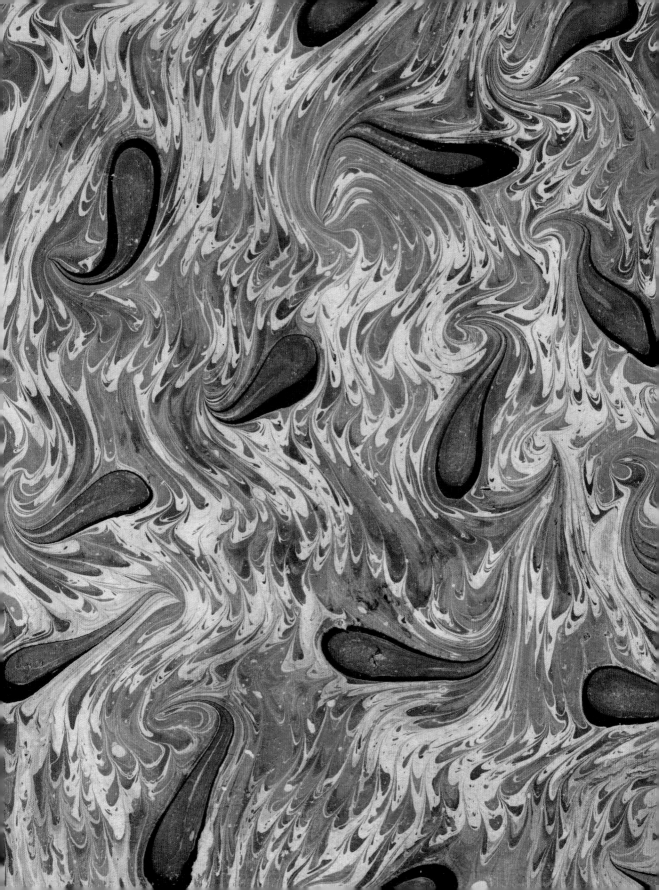

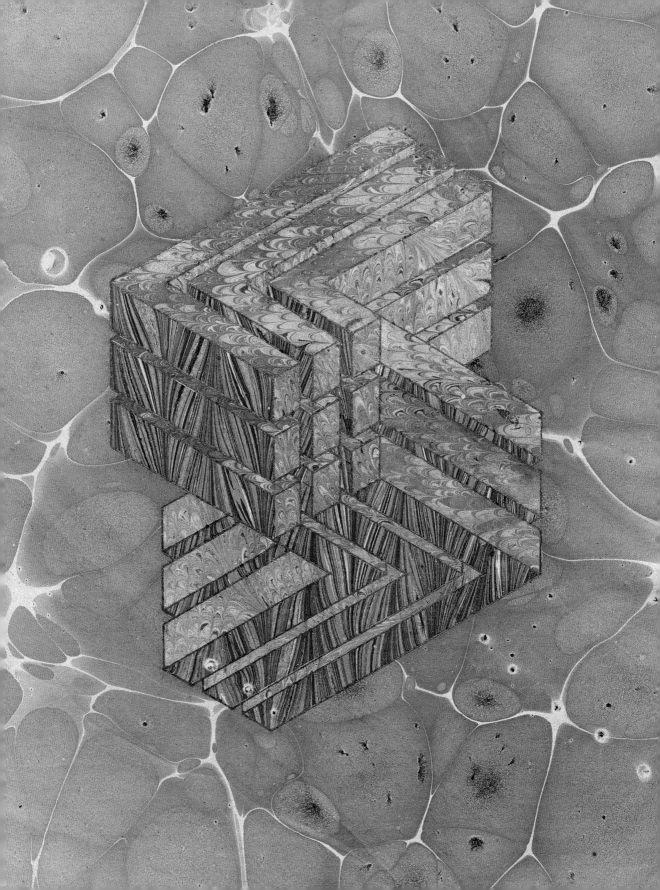

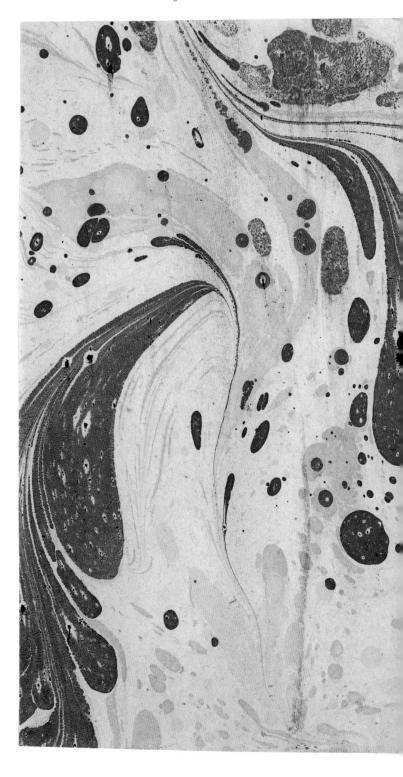

Page 56
Twentieth-century European marbling, involving sprinkling, combing and the use of a stylus. J.2042

Page 57
Twentieth-century English marbling by Graham Day. This pattern, part of Day's 'Integral Marbling' series, incorporates comb and chevron patterns on a background of stone marbling. Multiple resist techniques have also been used. Add.12

Right
Twentieth-century marbling probably made in Iran, where the name given to the technique, *abri*, translates as 'clouded paper'. J.3526

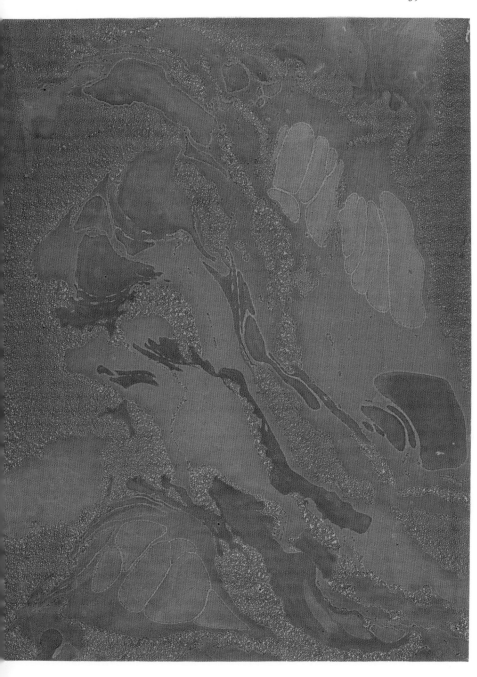

Above
Twentieth-century German
marbling in oils by Paul Kersten.
The technique used to produce this
pattern was not practised widely
until the publication of an article
by Kersten in 1904. According to
the paper historian Richard J.
Wolfe, the method became popular
because it produced 'quick and easy
results and now and then some
really interesting effects'. J.2031

Page 60
Twentieth-century European
comb marbling. J.2037

Page 61
Twentieth-century English comb
marbling by Cockerell & Son.
J.2051

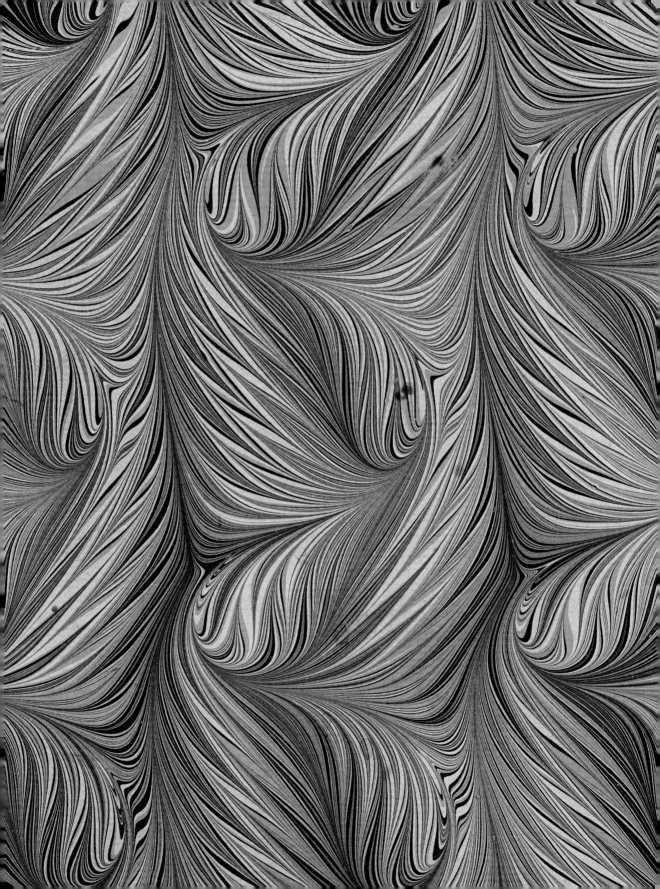

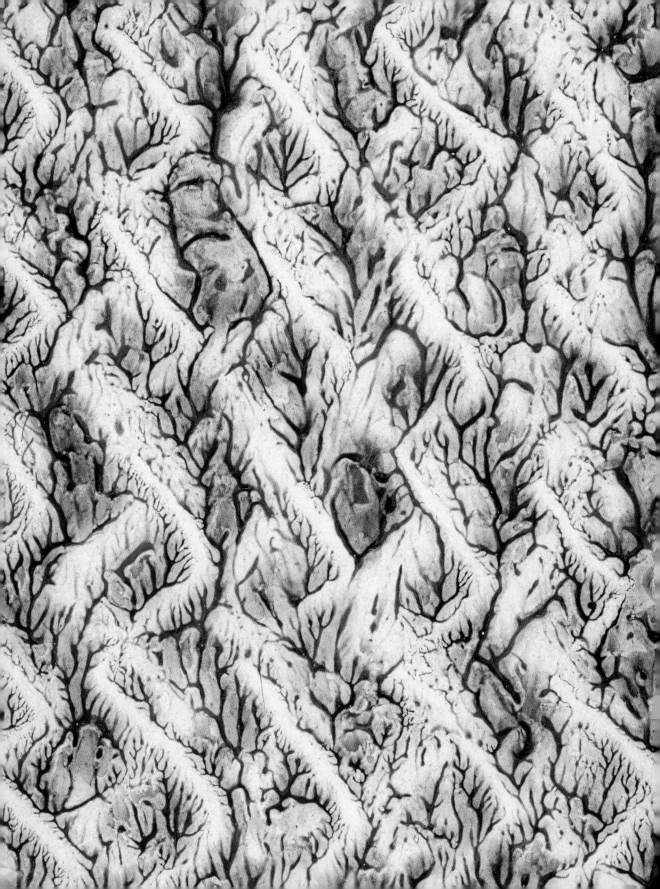

PASTE PAPERS

Paste papers can be made with few ingredients and little skill. A professional result, however, requires experience. Bookbinding apprentices were sometimes trained in their preparation.

Paste (usually derived from starch) is dyed with water-soluble colourants. Dyed paste is versatile, and decoration can be produced in a wide variety of ways, with brushes, fingers, styluses, stencils, sponges, combs, paper balls, string, engraved wheels – in fact, with just about anything you can lay your hands on (see fig. 1).

'Pulled' paste paper was a popular base style from the sixteenth century, and its use continues today.[1] A single-colour stippled paste-paper pattern (produced by placing a sheet of paper brushed with dyed paste face down on to a plain sheet and peeling it off immediately) provided a simple and cheap paper binding. More elaborate styles were created by using multiple colours and combining several techniques and tools.[2] Paste paper was often used to cover texts with relatively little bulk, such as music scores (see fig. 2), poetry collections, sermons and dissertations.

Although paste paper was in use in Europe by the end of the sixteenth century, it is frequently associated with the eighteenth-century Moravian religious community at Herrnhut in Germany, where it was made from 1764 to 1825.[3] Drawn designs in single-colour sheets of royal blue, red or olive green were popular with the sisters at Herrnhut. The technique was widespread throughout Europe, but particularly common in Germany, where it remained in use until the early twentieth century, when the Arts and Crafts Movement had a significant influence on its development.

Paste paper was a useful material for private presses. James H. Fraser notes that the Golden Hind Press in New Jersey (*fl.* 1927–55) used paste paper for covering its titles because 'its cheerful distinctiveness and economy of production are conducive to the needs of the printer-publisher'.[4]

Fig. 1: Single-coloured brushed paste paper with a diaper-shaped framework of flowers and foliage and central dabs of colour. J.2374

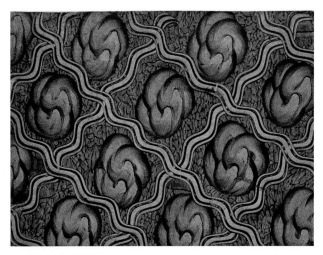

Fig. 3: Nineteenth- to twentieth-century European single-coloured veined paste paper with the veins travelling in alternating directions. J.2321

Fig. 2: Eighteenth-century European music-score cover. Veined paste paper with a diaper-shaped framework of wavy lines enclosing dabs of colour. J.2276.a

Modern artists have recognized the potential of paste paint by incorporating contemporary colourants, including acrylic and metallic. The latter in particular is popular with the American artist Claire Maziarczyk.

Paste papers are distinguished by intense colour, vivacity and a three-dimensional quality (see fig. 3). Moreover, they provide the paper-maker with an outlet for individual expression that, in the most inspired examples, can result in a momentary dialogue between the viewer and the practitioner.

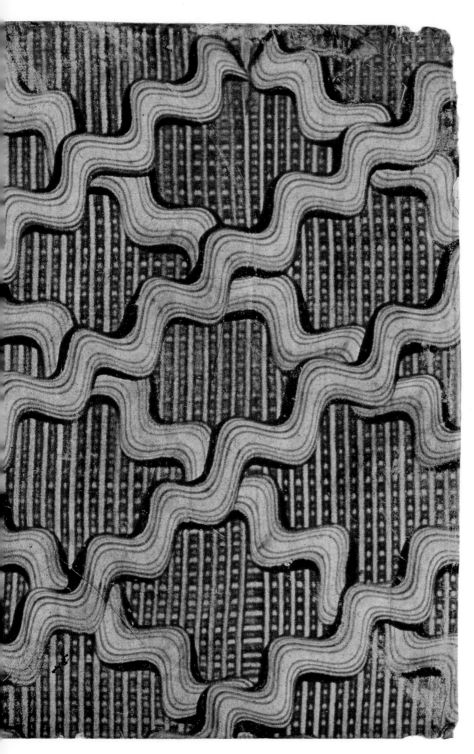

Left
Eighteenth-century European paste paper with impressed decoration. A lattice base has been covered with a wide, wavy net of lines. J.2278

Page 66
Nineteenth-century European brushed paste paper (*c.* 1800–10). The technique used here represents a relatively fast means of decorating paper. A variety of effects could be obtained by using brushes of different shapes. J.2253

Page 67
Twentieth-century German paste paper by Lilli Behrens (1869–1959). Together with her husband, the architect and typographer Peter Behrens, she exhibited at the St Louis World's Fair of 1904. Her contribution to the German pavilion was catalogued as 'coloured paper from Düsseldorf'. J.2569

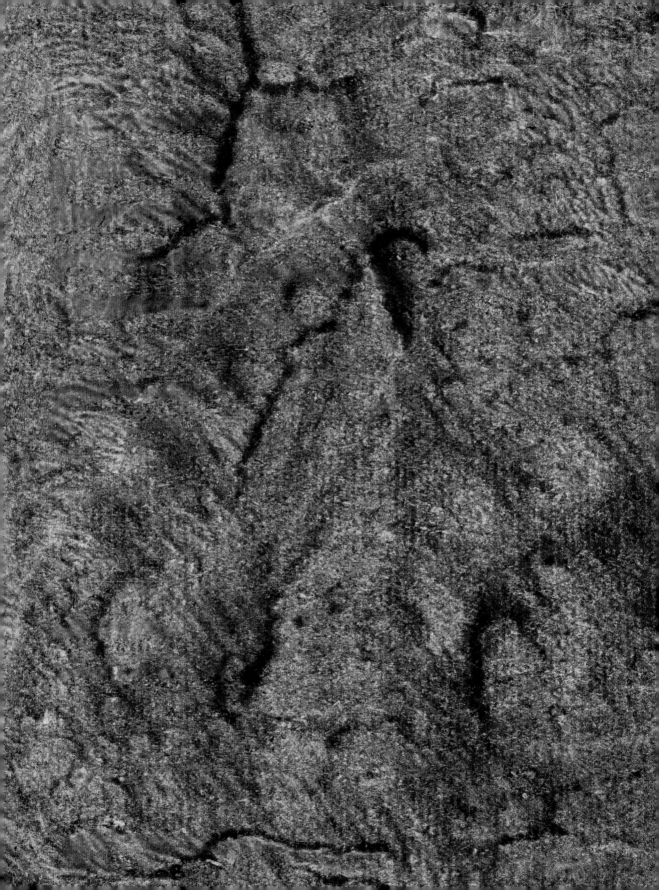

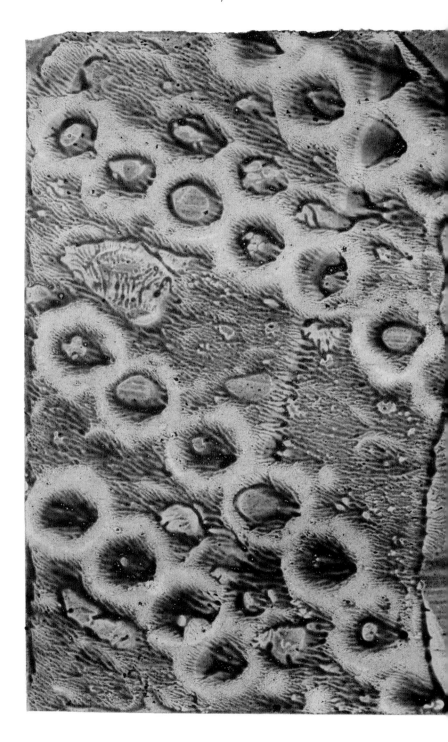

Page 68
Eighteenth-century northern
European veined paste paper.
J.2302

Page 69
Twentieth-century German paste
paper by Renate Hirsch (1917–
1983), Frankfurt am Main. Renate
was the daughter of the decorated-
paper collector Olga Hirsch. J.2651

Right
Twentieth-century German paste
paper by Renate Hirsch, Frankfurt
am Main. To produce the mirror-
image pattern, the paper was
brushed with paste paint, loosely
folded, pressed from the underside
using circular and diagonal
movements, and opened out.
J.2681

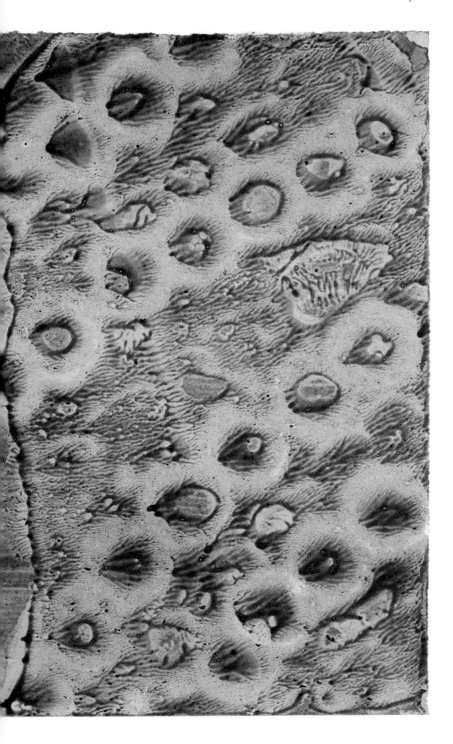

Page 72
Nineteenth-century European veined paste paper in four colours. The design has been applied using a carved block. J.2386

Page 73
Twentieth-century German paste paper by Paul Kersten (1905). J.2547

Pages 74–5
Twentieth-century German paste paper by Renate Hirsch, Frankfurt am Main (1934). In this example, the paper has been brushed with paste paint and dabbed with a dry material, such as paper crumpled into a ball. J.2669

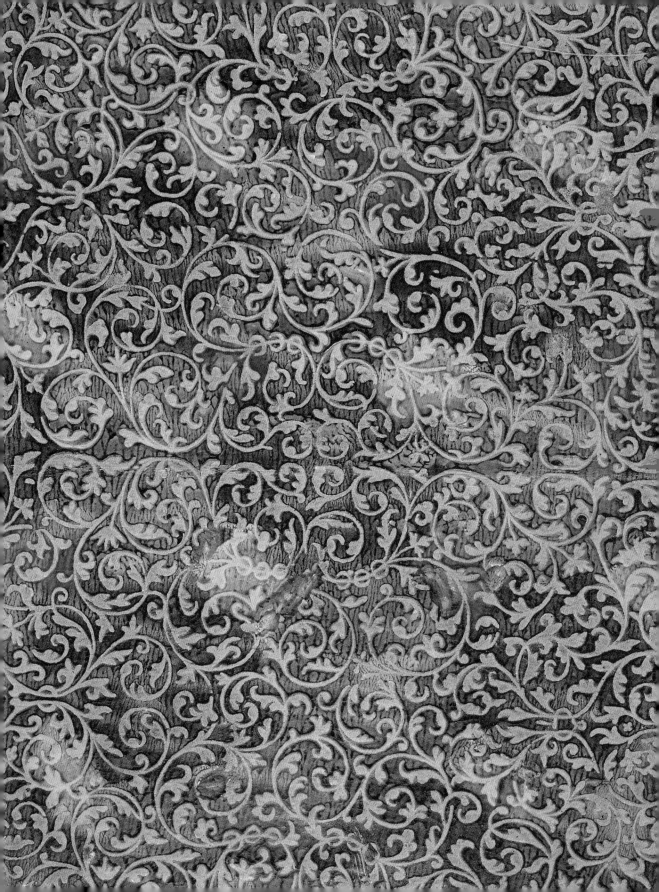

Above and opposite
These three examples demonstrate
the versatility of paste paint.
The exuberant north European
design (*c.* 1765–80; above) has been
drawn into wet paste paint with
a variety of implements, probably
including a comb. The backgrounds
of the two twentieth-century
European papers (opposite, top
and bottom) have been brushed.
J.2288, J.2738, J.2642

Page 78
Nineteenth-century European
diagonally brushed paste paper
(*c.* 1800–10). The application
of paste paint using a brush
can be quickly accomplished but
nevertheless produces a dramatic
effect due to the pronounced
gradations of colour. J.2254

Page 79
Twentieth-century German
paste paper by Renate Hirsch,
Frankfurt am Main (1932). Here,
the background looks as though
it has been applied with a brush.
Dabs of paint have been added
subsequently. J.2664

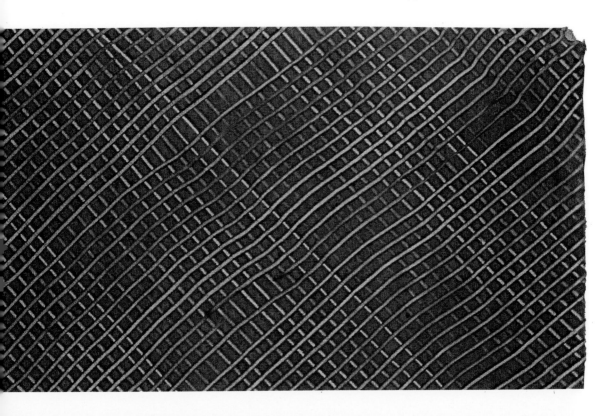

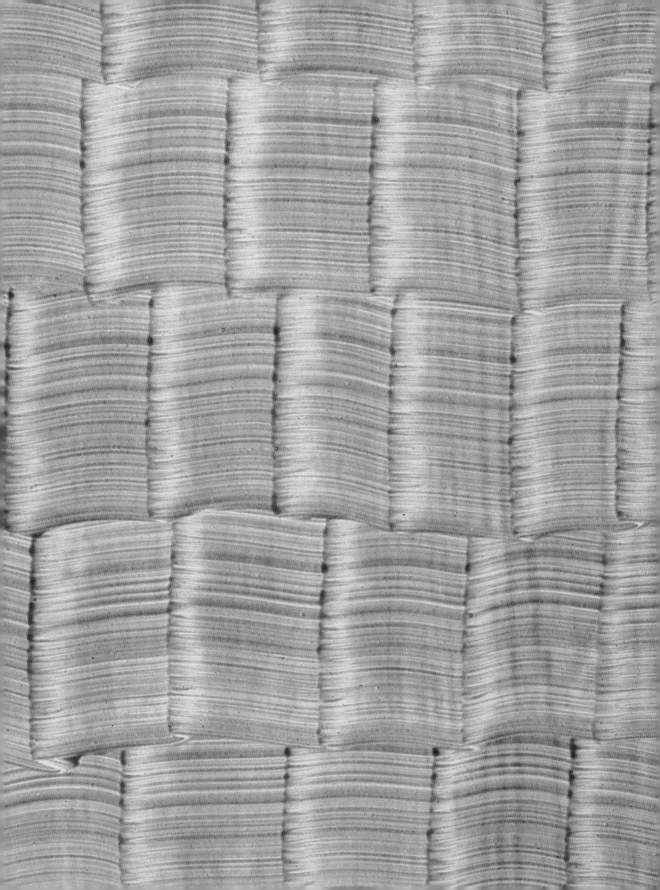

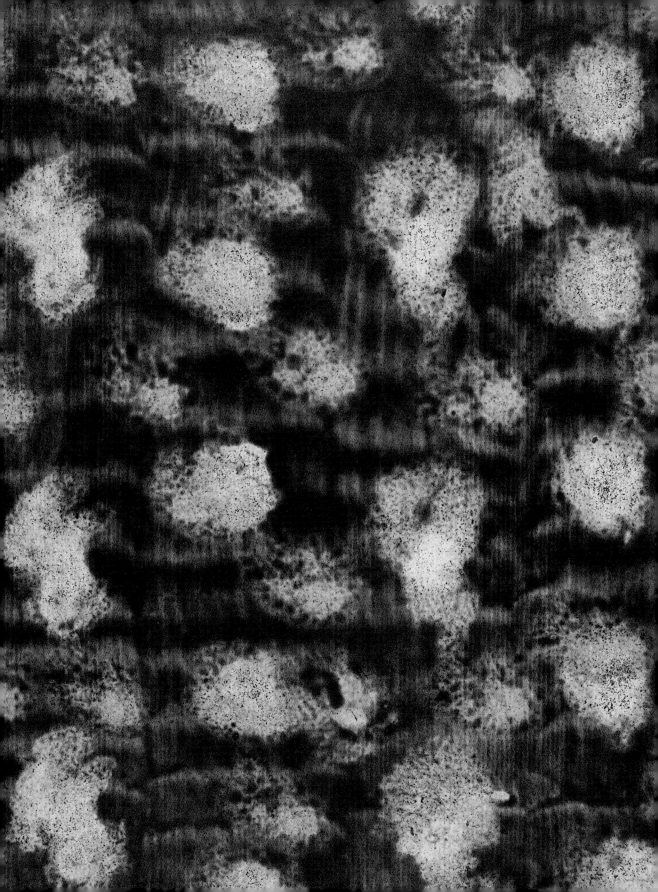

Page 80
Twentieth-century British paste
paper with brushed decoration
by Victoria Hall. Add.15.(7)

Page 81
Twentieth-century German paste
paper by Renate Hirsch, Frankfurt
am Main (1932). J.2663

Right
Twentieth-century European
paste paper, probably brushed
and blocked. J.2689

Page 84
Twentieth-century German paste
paper by Paul Kersten (1905). It is
not quite clear how this decoration
was achieved, although it is possible
that the paints were combined
with chemical additives. J.2563

Page 85
Twentieth-century European
paste paper. The diagonal strokes
and smears have been achieved
using several techniques. There
is evidence of brushwork, and
the circular smudges of colour
may have been transferred using
a sponge. J.2585

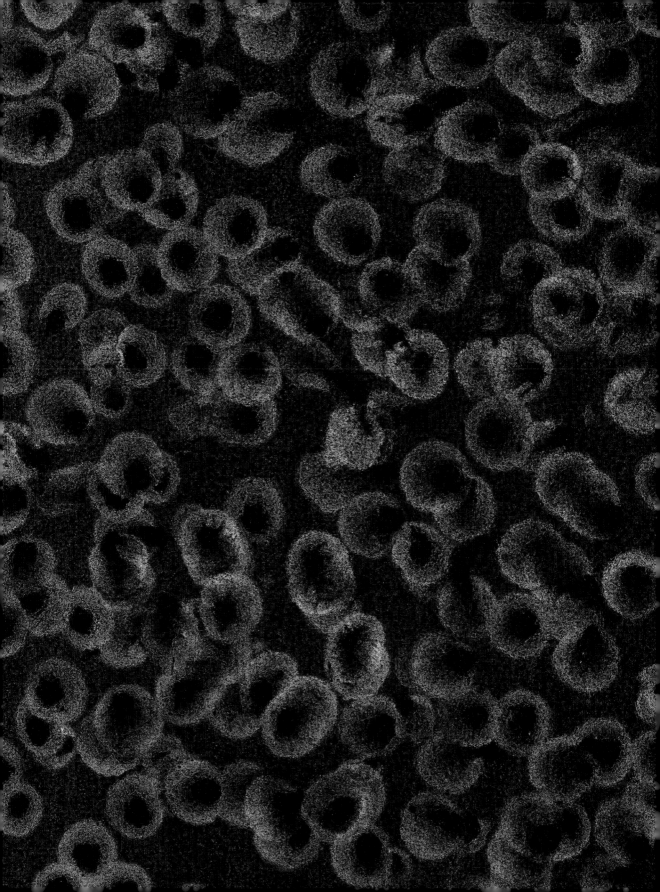

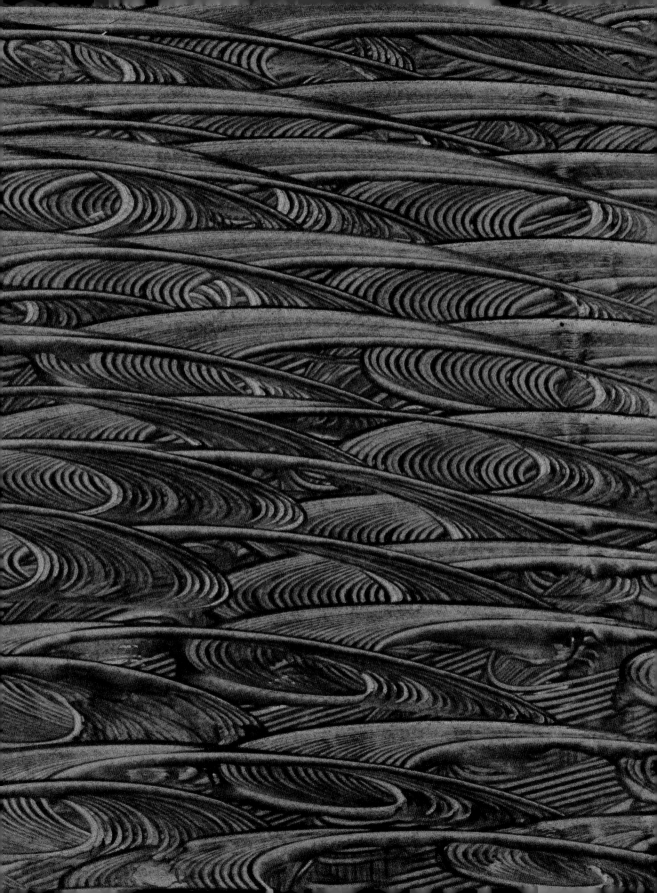

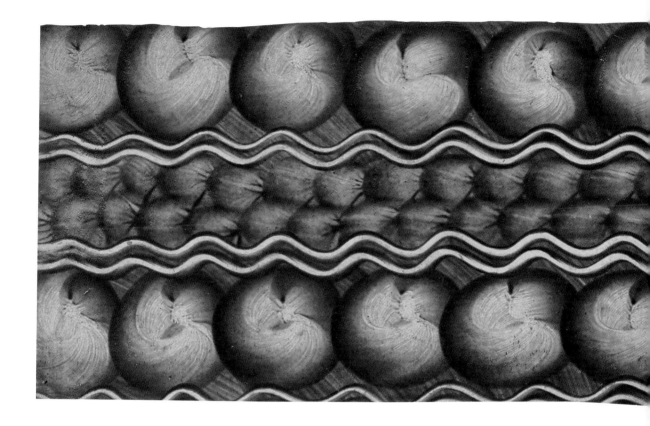

Above and opposite, bottom
Eighteenth-century north European
paste papers. Shades of blue, red and
green were commonly used for this
style, which has been associated with
a Moravian religious community
of paper-decorators in Herrnhut,
Germany, which flourished in the
late eighteenth century. The circular
daubs seen opposite (sometimes
made with the decorator's finger or
thumb) give a three-dimensional
effect. J.2354, J.2285

Opposite, top
This north European brown
veined paste paper (1765–80) gives
the impression of a less studied
composition. The decoration had
to be applied relatively swiftly,
as a dry surface would not
have received the impression
so effectively. J.2289

Pages 86 and 87
Twentieth-century German
combed paste papers by
Paul Kersten (1905). Note the
differences in outcome despite
the use of similar colours and
techniques. J.2538, J.2546

Pages 90 and 91
Twentieth-century German paste
papers by Eduard Ludwig (1906–
1960), architect and member of the
Bauhaus group. The pale, delicate
floral pattern seems particularly
suited to the thin paper that has
been used. The more dynamic,
almost calligraphic curls drawn
into the red-coloured paste provide
a dramatic contrast. J.2683, J.2685

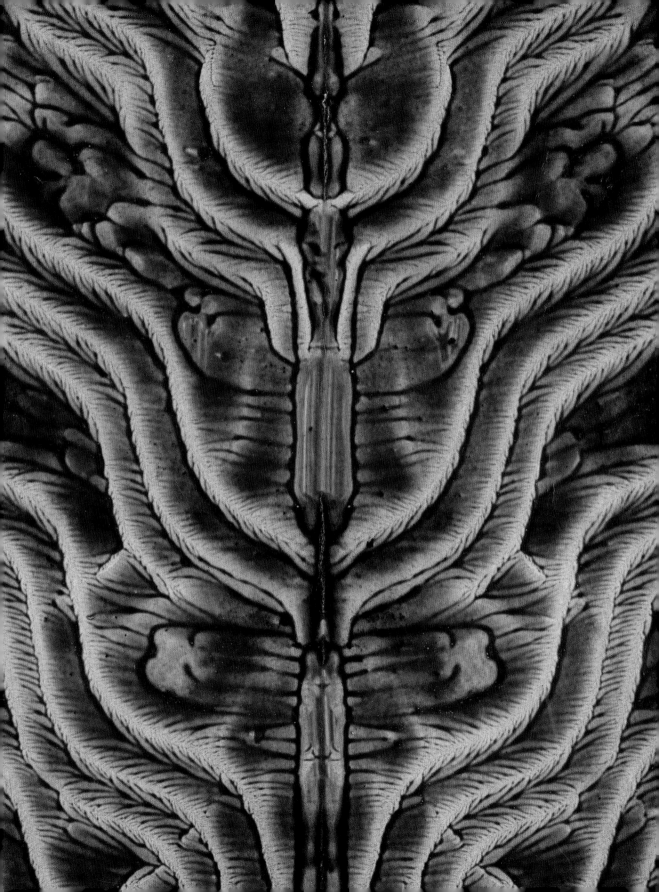

Pages 92 and 93
Twentieth-century German paste
papers by Paul Kersten (1905).
The Art of the Book, edited by
Charles Holme and published
in 1914, notes that 'Among the
professional craftsmen who yielded
to the new ideas of book production
Paul Kersten is perhaps the best
known, as he is without doubt
the most successful.' J.2543, J.2541

Opposite, top and bottom
Twentieth-century European
paste papers. J.2634, J.2635

Above
Twentieth-century German
veined paste paper by Renate
Hirsch, Frankfurt am Main (1932).
This style has been in use since
the eighteenth century. J.2660

Pages 96–7
Twentieth-century German
paper by Paul Kersten (1905).
It is difficult to distinguish the
techniques used, but it is likely
that blue paste paint has been
brushed on to the surface
and contrasting colours trickled
on top. J.2555

BROCADE PAPERS

Historically, papers decorated with gold or silver implied opulence, but the use of alloys rather than precious metals meant that luxury was affordable. The use of metals for embossing paper flourished in eighteenth- to nineteenth-century Germany, most notably in the states of Augsburg and Nuremberg between 1800 and 1850. The papers were widely traded; one highly decorated style, with multi-coloured floral motifs in relief, became known as 'Dutch gilt' (see fig. 1). This technique was frequently combined with stencilling, blocking and the application of different pigments and varnishes. Many brocade papers survive to this day – as covers for music scores or dissertations, and as end-leaves in printed books – providing a testament to the resilience of this type of decorated paper.

Bronze varnish papers are often mentioned alongside brocade papers because they feature similar motifs and emerged in Germany at roughly the same time (with the varnish papers appearing a little earlier). In fact, the two processes are completely different. Brocade papers feature a relief design, while bronze varnish papers involve block printing and are distinguished by a smooth surface. Brocade papers were made by heating an engraved brass plate. This was then coated with an alloy of metals and pressed on to the surface of coloured or plain paper via a rolling press (see figs 2 and 3). Elements of the surface design were raised, cut in either positive or negative relief.

Competition between workshops, which were often run as family businesses, was fierce, and successful designs were protected. The engraved plates were traded too, the new owner inserting his own name in the border in place of the original. A cheaper way of acquiring a design was simply to copy it, although the pattern would appear in reverse. Trade could also be furthered through marriage. In 1703, Georg Christoph Stoy's betrothal to Anna Barbara Enderlin, the sister of Jacob Enderlin (producer of bronze varnish papers) and the widow of

Fig. 1: An eighteenth-century brocade paper of the type sometimes known as 'Dutch gilt'. The name may be a misinterpretation of 'Deutsch'. J.81

Mathias Fröhlich (an Augsburg painter and maker of decorated papers), eventually gained Stoy not only a wife but also a business and an imperial privilege.[1]

Decoration included flowers and foliage, educational motifs (alphabets and numbers), religious scenes, and aspects of contemporary life (such as crafts, national dress and hunting; see figs 4 and 5, and pages 106–7, 109, 111, 117, 122–3, 128–9 and 131). Brocade papers decorated in this way were known as *Bilderbogen* (picture sheets).

From the late 1700s, the artistic quality of the decoration deteriorated.[2] Brocade papers lingered, however, and were used as ornate but inexpensive bindings for books intended to be given as presents or school prizes. The French publisher A. Mame et Cie of Tours specialized in this type of binding (see fig. 6).

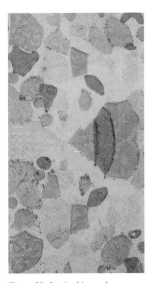

Fig. 2: Unfinished brocade paper, probably used as a proof to demonstrate the placing of the stencilled colours. The background design is only just visible. J.78

Fig. 3: Detail from an eighteenth-century German brocade paper by Johann Michael Schwibecher (*fl. c.* 1715–48) of Augsburg. Note the three-dimensional quality of the surface. J.218

Fig. 4: Detail from a German brocade design (probably early nineteenth century) on plain coloured paper by Paul Reimund (*fl.* 1783–1815). J.307

Fig. 5: Nineteenth-century German brocade paper celebrating the inaugural railway journey from Nuremberg to Fürth in December 1835. The cheerful colours somewhat obscure the images of the train. J.313

Fig. 6: Lower cover of a nineteenth-century gift book published by A. Mame et Cie (Abbé Guerinet, *Paul, ou Les dangers d'un caractère faible*, Tours, 1858). BJ.21 [3]

Left
Eighteenth-century European
varnish paper featuring silver
carnations on a pink background.
Varnish papers have a flatter surface
than brocade papers, and were
invented slightly earlier. J.15

Page 102
Eighteenth-century German
brocade paper featuring
floral gold embossing over red
paste paper, signed by Johann
Carl Munck (*fl.* 1750–94)
of Augsburg. J.119

Page 103
Nineteenth-century German
brocade paper inscribed with a
phrase that translates as 'Dwarf
Society'. The figures are drinking,
taking snuff and smoking. The
Hirsch collection also contains
examples of this design on purple
and orange painted backgrounds.
J.312

Page 104
Eighteenth-century German brocade paper (*c.* 1740). The gold may have tarnished, causing the pattern to darken over time. J.186

Page 105
Eighteenth-century German brocade paper with chinoiserie motifs (*c.* 1730). Mirjam Foot notes that 'the influence of the Far East on art during the eighteenth century had also reached the German paper-decorators'. J.212

Above
Nineteenth-century brocade paper by Renner & Abel of Nuremberg (*c.* 1840). Sheets with motifs signifying letters (e.g. 'A' for 'Arabian horse') may have been seen as more effective learning tools than simple 'ABC' panels. J.321

Opposite
Nineteenth-century German brocade paper (1800–50) by Renner & Abel of Nuremberg. It depicts Adam and Eve at the Tree of Knowledge surrounded by pairs of exotic and domestic animals. J.298

Page 108
Eighteenth-century German
stencilled brocade paper. The
gold is raised above the surface
of the sheet. J.93

Page 109
Nineteenth-century German
brocade paper signed in the lower
border 'Johann Paul Schindler
[c. 1750–1814], Fürth'. The pattern,
a floral design in gold alloy on
purple paste paper, is no. 8 in
Schindler's stock book. J.130

Page 110
Eighteenth-century German
brocade paper, probably by David
Mehrer (1685–1747) of Augsburg.
J.45

Page 111
Eighteenth-century German
brocade paper featuring a variety
of animals. The bold diagonal
stripes of paste paint tend to
obscure the details, but the paper's
motifs and bright appearance would
have been particularly attractive
to a child. J.63

Above
Eighteenth-century German
brocade-paper wrapper, probably
made in Augsburg. The pattern
may have been produced first by
Simon Haichele (*fl.* 1740–50) and
subsequently by Johann Carl
Munck: the engraved brass plates
were valuable and commonly traded
between craftsmen. J.216

Page 114
Eighteenth-century German
brocade paper signed 'Maerckli'
(probably Mattheus Merktl of
Augsburg, *fl.* 1730–52). Merktl
purchased a licence to produce
gold and silver papers from a
pioneer of embossing, Abraham
Mieser (1690–1742). J.141

Page 115
Eighteenth-century German
brocade paper (1715–20) by
Georg Christoph Stoy. Note
the half-concealed dog, deer
and birds. J.199

Nineteenth-century German
brocade paper attributed to
Johann Georg Eckart (*fl.* 1820–54)
of Nuremberg. It seems likely,
owing to the nature of the design,
that Eckart copied it from Paul
Reimund. J.319

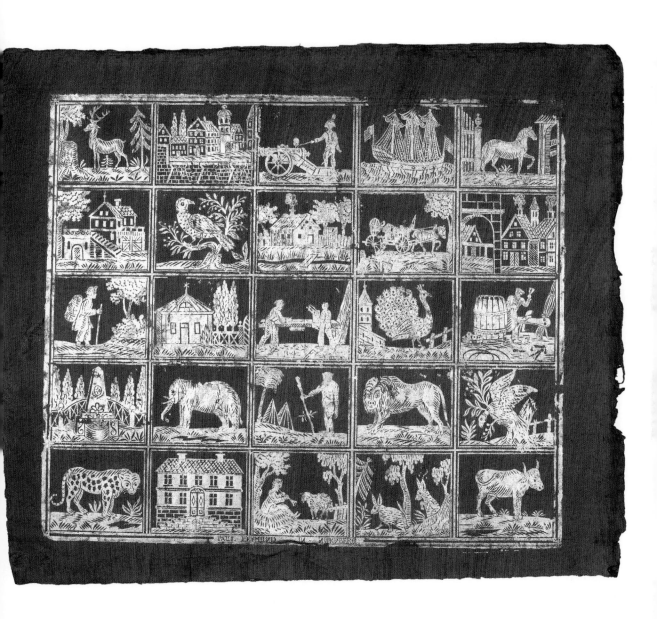

Above
Eighteenth- to nineteenth-century
German brocade paper in silver
by Paul Reimund of Nuremberg.
The images, including a soldier
firing a cannon, a wild man, exotic
animals and a galleon, may have
appealed to schoolboys. J.281

Pages 118–19
Eighteenth-century German
brocade paper (*c.* 1750–60).
The paint overlaying the gold
embossing may have been added
with the use of a stencil. J.55

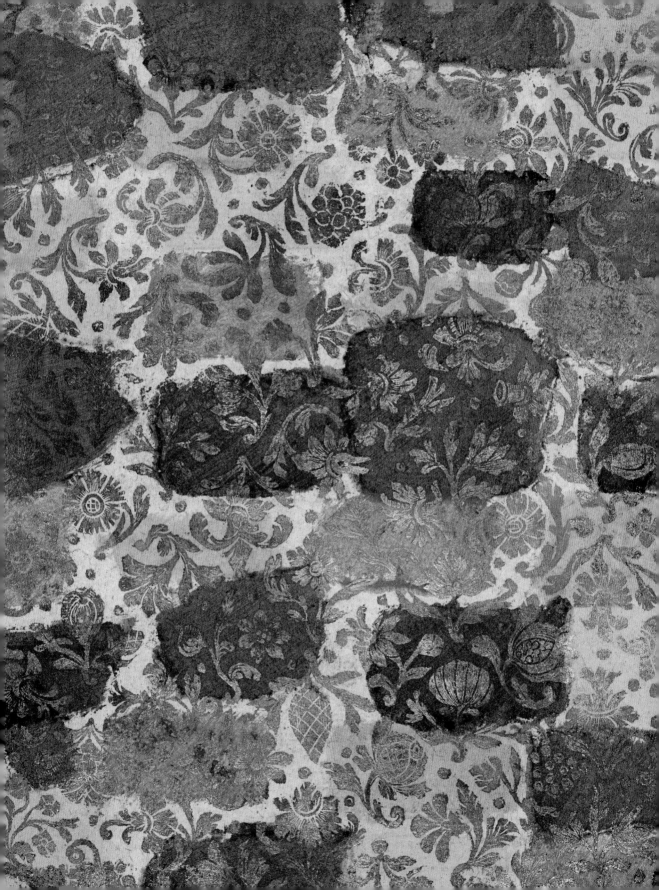

Page 120
Eighteenth-century German brocade paper with a floral design on purple paper by Paul Reimund. Reimund's grandfather Johann Michael, his father, Andreas, and his younger brother, Georg Daniel, were all in the trade. After Reimund's death in 1815, his widow continued the business. J.123

Page 121
Eighteenth-century German brocade paper. The flowers have been embossed on to a plain background; the patches of red, purple, orange and yellow were probably added using a stencil. J.84

Right
Eighteenth-century German brocade paper. Olga Hirsch suggested that this design, which features the Nativity from the New Testament, is the reverse of pattern no. 64 by Johann Michael Munck of Augsburg. This implies that Munck's paper was copied. J.240

Page 124
Eighteenth-century German brocade paper, gold on a white ground, probably made in Augsburg. This was a common pattern and appears in papers by Joseph Friedrich Leopold (*c.* 1669–1727) and Johann Wilhelm Meyer (*fl.* 1740–80) of Augsburg, and by Johann Lechner of Fürth. J.205

Page 125
Eighteenth-century German brocade paper, unidentified. Georg Christoph Stoy is known to have printed on similar dark-red backgrounds. J.222

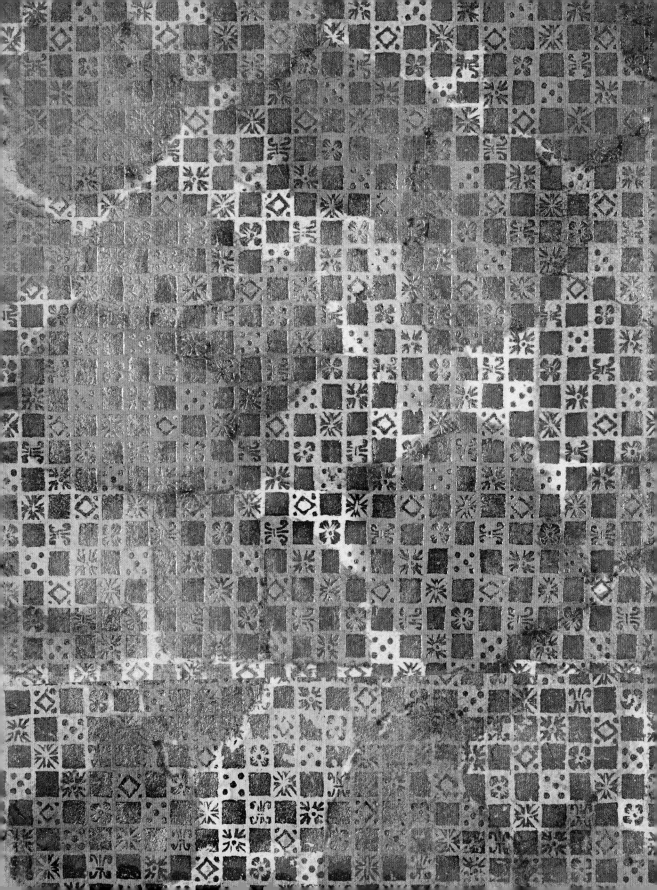

Page 126
Eighteenth-century German
brocade paper. Here, the gold
embossing has been set against
a plain-green background. J.171

Page 127
Eighteenth-century German
brocade paper with flowers and
birds blocked on to a gold-coloured
background. The blocks of blue,
yellow, orange and red paint were
added by means of a stencil. J.85

Above
Eighteenth-century German
brocade paper, unidentified. Saints
were popular subjects, and often
featured on a range of coloured
backgrounds (see also J.268,
opposite). J.267

Opposite
Eighteenth-century German
brocade paper, unidentified.
This is a version of J.267 (above),
but has been embossed on
a brown background. J.268

Page 130
Eighteenth-century German
brocade paper on a green
background. Patterned textiles
often featured similar motifs.
J.178

Page 131
Nineteenth-century German
brocade paper depicting twelve
countryside scenes, each one
illustrating a different month
of the calendar. J.306

BLOCK-PRINTED PAPERS

Many block-printed papers can be characterized by the idiom 'cheap and cheerful', since the technique is relatively simple and inexpensive. A woodblock covered with viscous paint is pressed on to single sheets of paper. A multi-coloured design requires a separate block and a separate pressing for each shade.

Regional differences arose both in style and method. China adopted block printing relatively early, using it, for example, for the famous 'Diamond Sutra' of AD 868. The basic process spread throughout East Asia and Europe in the thirteenth century. In the Far East, the block was placed with the carved face upwards and the paper lying on top. An implement of some kind was then passed across the verso of the sheet to press it on to the block, a technique known as rubbing. In Europe, the craftsman would press the block downwards on to the paper. In Japan, the traditional method persisted even after the fifteenth century, when the printing press presented a more economic means of transfer.

More expensive kinds of block-printed papers were also produced, such as bronze varnish papers, which first appeared in Germany between 1685 and 1692 (see fig. 1). Varnish-based metallic ink or a lacquer mixed with a powdered metal (e.g. bronze, copper, silver or brass) was applied to a woodblock. This was then pressed on to a sheet of decorated paper until the surface had been covered, each print requiring a new application of the varnish or paint to the block.

European block-makers often hammered metal pins or strips into the block. These added to the design a background of dots or thin lines. Known as 'picotage', the technique was also used in the decoration of fabric. The type of medium used – whether ink, thick or thin paint, paste paint, etc. – can also have an impact on the finished paper.

The function of block-printed papers was to add colour and vibrancy, for example to poorly lit dwellings or cheap, mass-market books. Bold designs were needed, but not necessarily detail. Less elaborate patterns, such as circles, stars or stripes, did not require an experienced woodcarver but were popular nonetheless.[1] The paper decorators knew the requirements of their market. In eighteenth-century Italy, the Remondini family printed sheets of motifs (flowers, animals, figures in exotic dress), which could be cut out individually, pasted on to household objects (containers, hair brushes, etc.) and varnished for protection. This practice also occurred in Japan.

In Japan, the most colourful manifestation of block printing was *chiyogami*, a style that flourished between the seventeenth and nineteenth centuries in Tokyo, Kyoto and Osaka. Sheets were decorated with educational themes, multi-coloured plants and animals, auspicious motifs, and emblems taken from classic stories and plays (see fig. 2).[2] *Chiyogami* was cheaper to produce and viewed as less sophisticated than single sheets

Fig. 1: Detail of an eighteenth-century German bronze varnish paper depicting soldiers ensnared by foliage. Note the smooth surface. J.9

decorated in another contemporary style, the higher-class *ukiyo-e*. According to Ann Herring, *chiyogami* retained its vitality owing to a 'successful combination of classicism and conventionality with timelessness and the ability to adapt to new circumstances'.3

Block printing was practised in Europe and the Far East until the nineteenth century, when it was superseded by techniques that employed mass production. These included lithography and screen-printing, which is commonly used for *chiyogami* today.

Fig. 2: Nineteenth-century Japanese crane motif associated with wedding ceremonies and the Japanese New Year. J.3455

Page 135
A late nineteenth- to mid-twentieth-century example of the Japanese style of block printing known as *chiyogami*. Maple leaves were a popular subject, and were associated with balance and serenity. J.3510

Right
Nineteenth- to twentieth-century Italian block printing, probably by Giannini & Son, a family-owned bookbinding and paper-decorating business founded in Florence in 1856 and still trading today. The firm uses traditional patterns and methods; the papers, for example, are blocked by hand. The fleur-de-lis motif is associated with Florence. J.1297

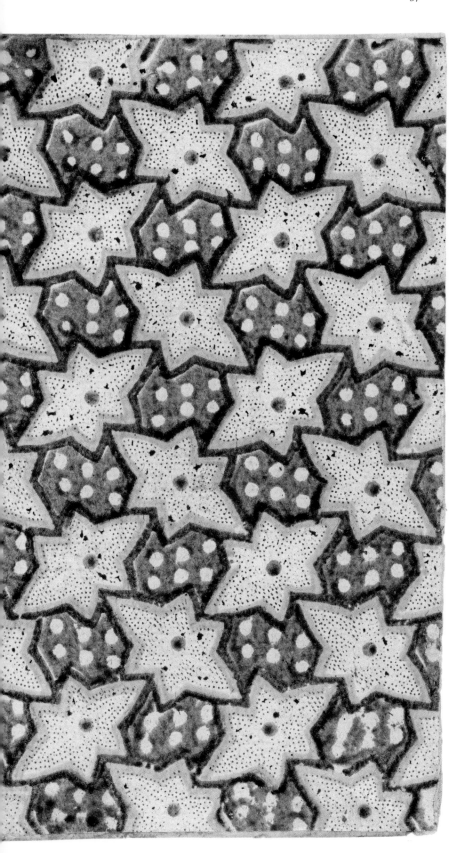

Left
Early to mid-nineteenth-century
block printing, probably Italian,
in blue and orange on a white
background. This popular motif
was also used in combination with
other colours. J.722

Page 138
Nineteenth- to twentieth-century
Chinese block printing featuring
birds and foliage. J.3469

Page 139
Nineteenth-century German block
printing (*c.* 1830–70). This type of
paper was useful for many common
household purposes, including the
wrapping of powdered medicines
and sugar. J.1182

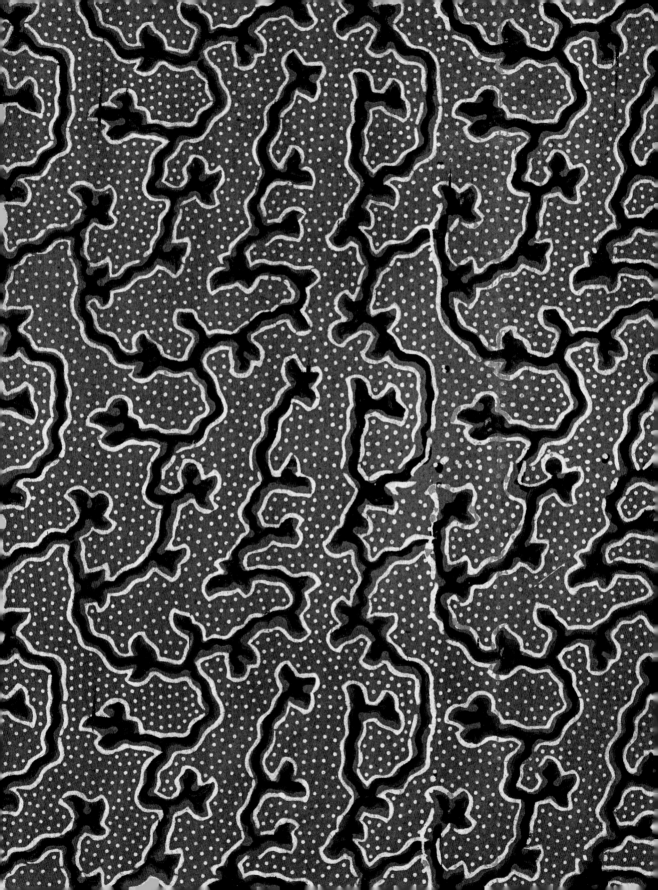

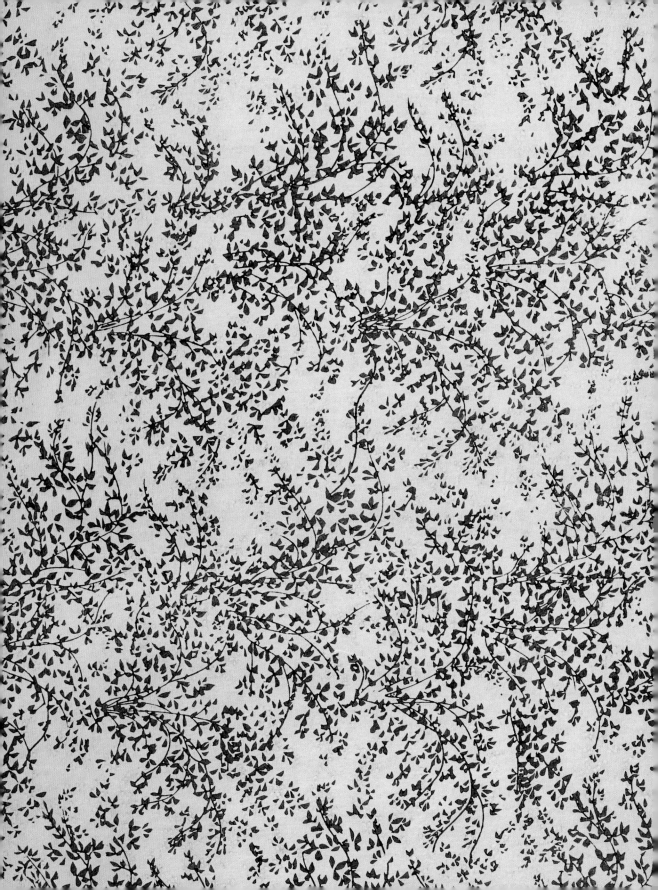

Pages 140 and 141
Two examples of late nineteenth-
to mid-twentieth-century
chiyogami. J.3438, J.3437

Right
Nineteenth- to twentieth-century
Italian block printing. The leaf
motif is reminiscent of paisley,
a pattern that is often used on
textiles. Writing about block
printing in his *Dictionary of the
Arts and Crafts* (*c.* 1770), Francesco
Griselini noted that 'the sheets
of paper are stamped in the fashion
of Indian cloth'. J.1294

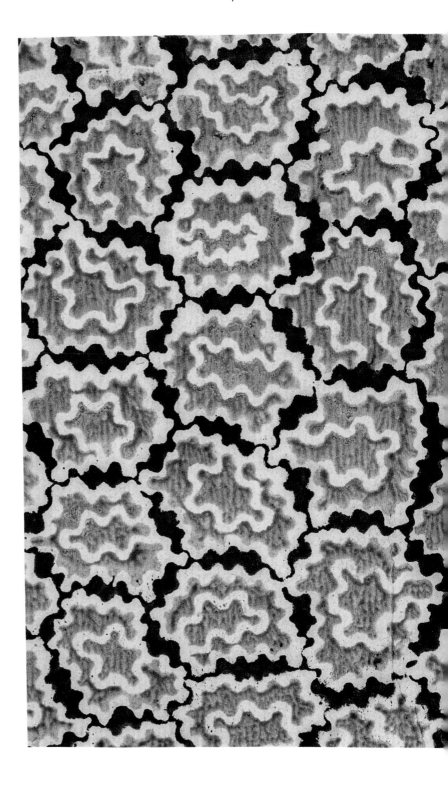

Page 148
A twentieth-century example
of *chiyogami*. J.3446

Page 149
Nineteenth- to twentieth-century
Italian block printing. Part-time
Italian pedlars carried the papers
as far afield as Poland, Bohemia
and Russia. Their journeys began
in August and ended in early
spring, when the family farms
needed their attention. This type
of informal network had first arisen
at least as early as the sixteenth
century. J.1308

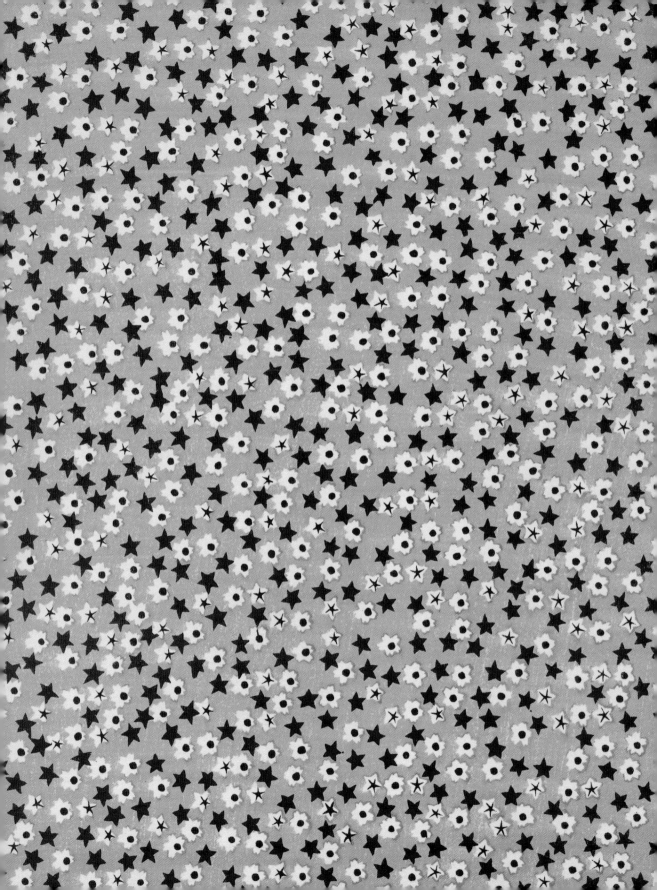

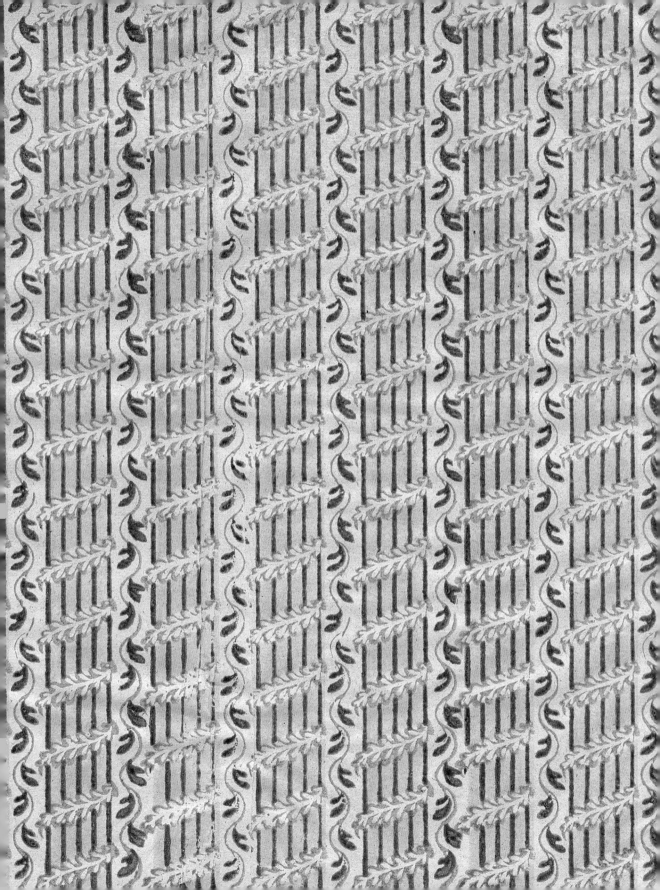

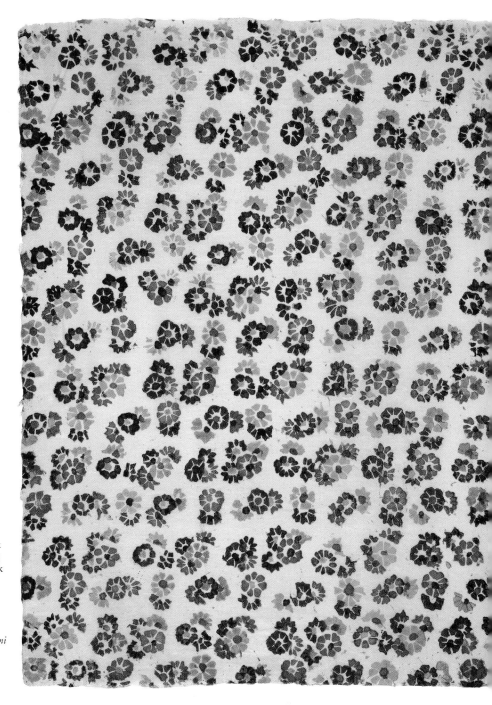

Page 150
Twentieth-century Italian block printing, probably created using a nineteenth-century woodblock from the historic Bassano firm of Remondini. J.1312

Page 151
Probably late nineteenth- to early twentieth-century *chiyogami* featuring coloured leaves, a common motif. In Japan, the viewing of autumn foliage, a tradition known as *momijigari*, is an important cultural activity. J.3409.a

Right
Nineteenth- to twentieth-century *chiyogami*. The style owed much to traditional subjects, which had specific meanings for the Japanese. Motifs were inspired by such natural phenomena as flowers, plants, butterflies and birds. J.3445

Left
Twentieth-century Far Eastern
block printing on crêpe paper.
J.3496

Page 154
Twentieth-century Chinese block
printing on very thin paper. J.3459

Page 155
Nineteenth- to twentieth-century
chiyogami. J.3432

Page 156
Probably late nineteenth-century
chiyogami. In accordance with
traditional Japanese culture, the
flowers depicted had a symbolic
meaning. The chrysanthemum
was the symbol of imperial Japan,
and red carnations suggested
romantic love. J.3409

Page 157
Eighteenth- to nineteenth-century
block printing in three colours.
The quality of the print indicates
that it was made by a skilled
practitioner. J.409

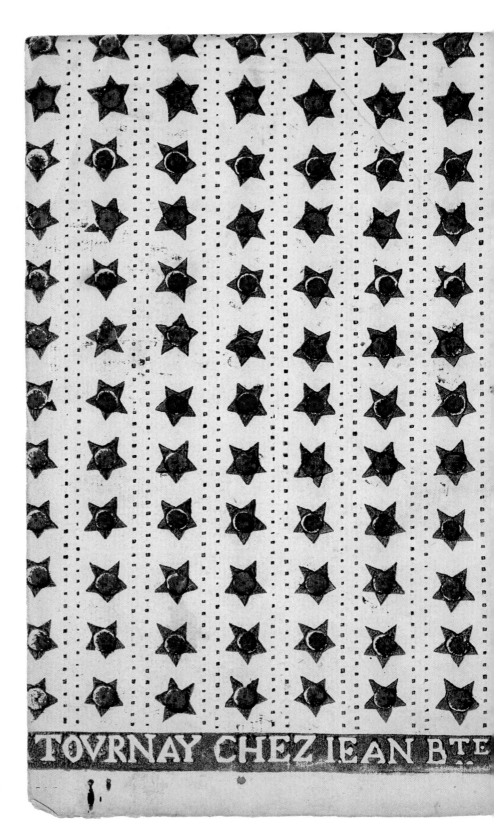

Eighteenth-century block printing by Jean-Baptiste Ghys of Tournai (Low Countries). Note the name and address in the lower border. J.1400

YS DANS LA RVE DE PONT

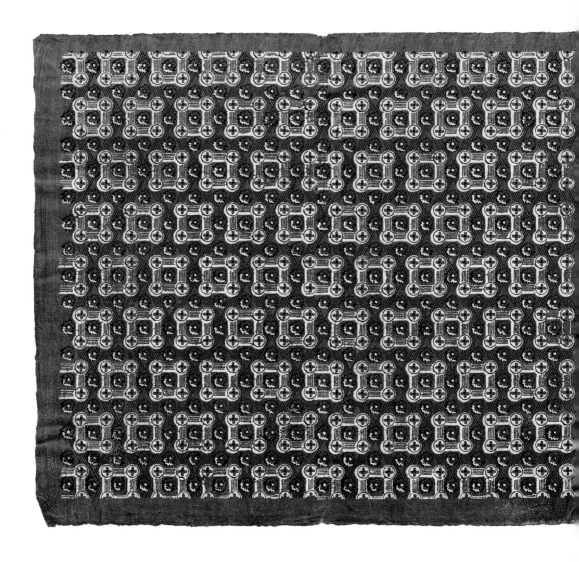

Page 160
Nineteenth-century German block printing (*c.* 1860–70). J.1172

Page 161
Eighteenth-century block printing by Jean-Baptiste Ghys of Tournai. Such bold yet simple repeat patterns were particularly effective, and were also produced by French and Italian paper-decorators. J.1399

Above and opposite
Nineteenth- to twentieth-century Italian block printing. The Italians had a sophisticated marketing operation. In his contribution to the edited volume *Not Dead Things: The Dissemination of Popular Print* (2013), the Italian print and decorated-paper author and researcher Alberto Milano notes that the 'well-articulated strategy was widespread distribution carried out by thousands of pedlars'. J.1318, J.1267

Page 164
Nineteenth- to twentieth-century *chiyogami* featuring wisteria, a plant associated in Japanese culture with longevity. J.3456

Page 165
Nineteenth- to twentieth-century Japanese block printing. To a Japanese audience, this wave-like pattern conveyed a sense of power and resilience. J.3428.a

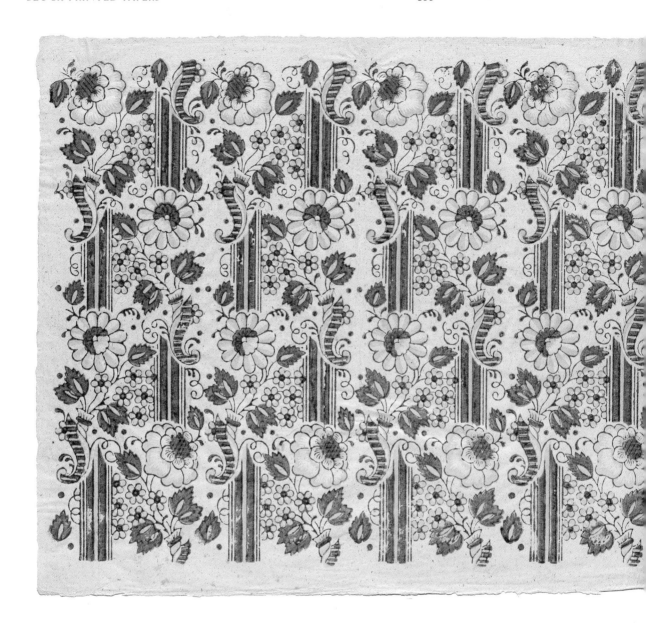

Page 166
Nineteenth-century block printing,
probably Japanese. Traditional
printing techniques were often
enhanced by the use of paper with
different textures. This example
showcases block printing on
crêpe paper. J.3498

Page 167
Eighteenth- to nineteenth-century
European block printing in a single
colour featuring floral and lace
motifs. In *Buntpapier*, Albert
Haemmerle uses the term 'cotton
paper' to describe this style. J.370

Above
Nineteenth- to twentieth-century
Italian block printing. The
optimistic quality of the design,
conveyed by the use of yellow,
is a characteristic of many
Italian styles. J.1310

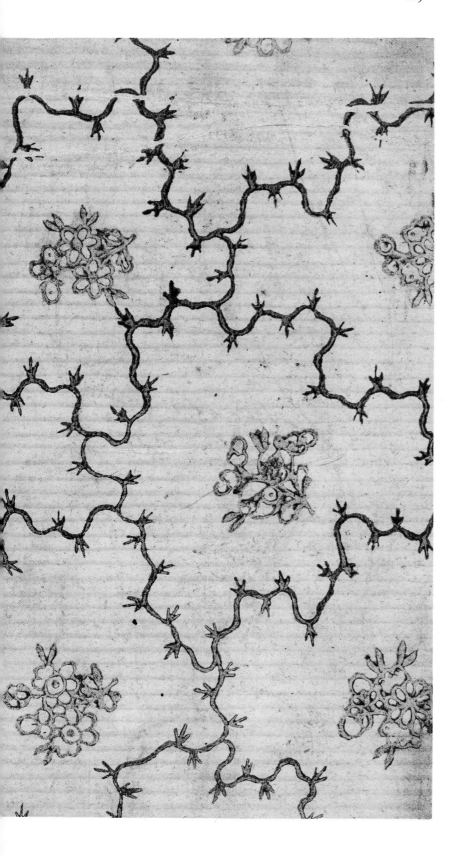

Eighteenth- to nineteenth-century
European block printing. It seems
likely that the colours have faded
with time. J.1012

MASS PRODUCTION

The Nineteenth Century and Beyond

In Europe, the 1800s saw the introduction of cheaper, mass-produced papers thanks to mechanization, which affected the Near and Far East markets approximately a century later. Traditional methods, notably letterpress printing, which employed woodblocks and a hand press (see fig. 1), faced competition. Techniques that yielded multiple copies simultaneously were enthusiastically adopted by workshop owners. Lithography, invented in Germany by Alois Senefelder in around 1796, was the first such technique. The process involves printing from a flat, inked surface (initially stone, later a metal plate) that has been treated so as to repel the ink except where it is required for printing (from 1860 power presses facilitated the process, and from the 1890s rotary presses

Fig. 1: Detail of a letterpress paper, *c.* 1830. J.2716

Fig. 2: Detail of a lithographic paper by Alois Dessauer, *c.* 1840. J.2787

Fig. 3: Child labour at a decorated-paper factory in nineteenth-century Aschaffenburg, Germany.

Fig. 4: An art nouveau-influenced design by Paul Kersten, Aschaffenburg, Germany, 1899. J.2789

Fig. 5: End-leaf from Catherine Franks (ed.), *The Pictorial Guide to Modern Home Knitting*, London, 1939. 07743.bb.1

hastened it).[1] Colour lithography followed, as did offset lithography, where the image is transferred to a rubber roller (or 'blanket') prior to printing.

An early producer of lithographed papers was Alois Dessauer's factory in Aschaffenburg, Germany (see fig. 2). The city was home to four leading printing firms, which between them employed more than a thousand people and manufactured a huge variety of decorated papers. These firms provided much-needed employment but often neglected the safety of their workers, many of whom were children (see fig. 3). There was also a concern that mechanization would adversely affect the originality of design. In 1837 the British government founded design schools not only to counter this concern but also to promote the often uncredited designers.

Gifted craftsmen, such as the teacher, writer and bookbinder Paul Kersten, were given the opportunity to experiment, in order to meet the demand for something new. Mechanization enabled designers to react quickly to new artistic developments (see fig. 4). Eventually, photomechanical printing, automated screen-printing (a type of stencilling) and, more recently, digitization joined lithography as quick and easy ways of producing decorated papers in large quantities. Automation also entered the world of marbling, allowing near-predictable patterns to be reproduced in bulk. Although this was tried by such firms as Cockerell & Son, it is difficult to differentiate between hand- and machine-marbled papers.

Printed end-leaves presented book publishers with an opportunity to add to the character of the text (see fig. 5) or to advertise their name. In late nineteenth-century America, the publishing houses of Henry Holt & Co., D. Appleton & Co. and J. B. Lippincott & Co. used patterns featuring their initials (see, for example, fig. 6).[2] In early twentieth-century England, such well-known artists as Edward Bawden, Enid Marx, Paul Nash, Eric Ravilious and Graham Sutherland often produced the initial designs for end-leaves, most notably for the Curwen Press (see fig. 7).[3]

The printing expert Stanley Morison commended lithography for the evenness of its printing, noting that 'the papers printed by hand from woodblocks, as made by Signor Rizzi of Varese, are less fit for commercial work'.[4] Paul Nash was of the opinion that lithographic reproduction was not 'truly mechanical', and that the 'hard, bright, resilient [Curwen] patterns are more in keeping with the modern spirit and admirably represent the revival in pattern paper production'.[5]

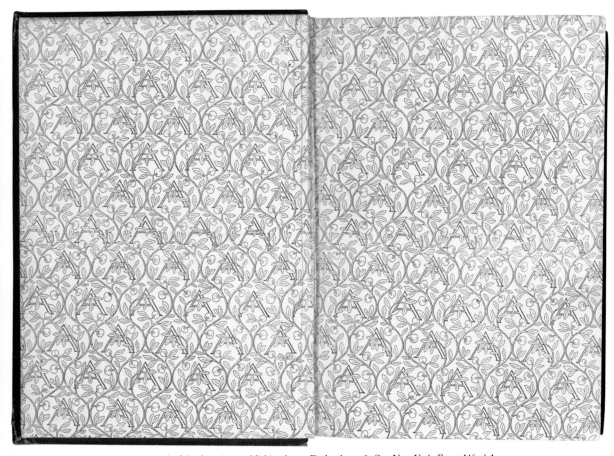

Fig. 6: End-leaf incorporating the initial of the American publishing house D. Appleton & Co., New York. From Alfred Ayres, *Acting and Actors, Elocution and Elocutionists*, 1894. 011805.de.2

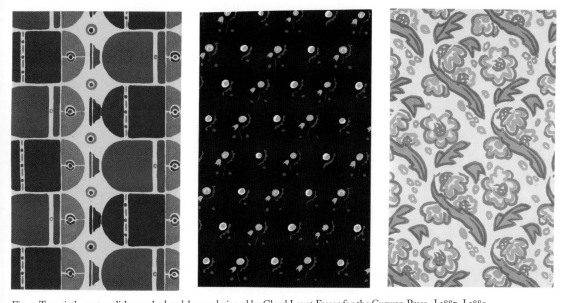

Fig. 7: Twentieth-century lithographed end-leaves designed by Claud Lovat Fraser for the Curwen Press. J.2887–J.2889

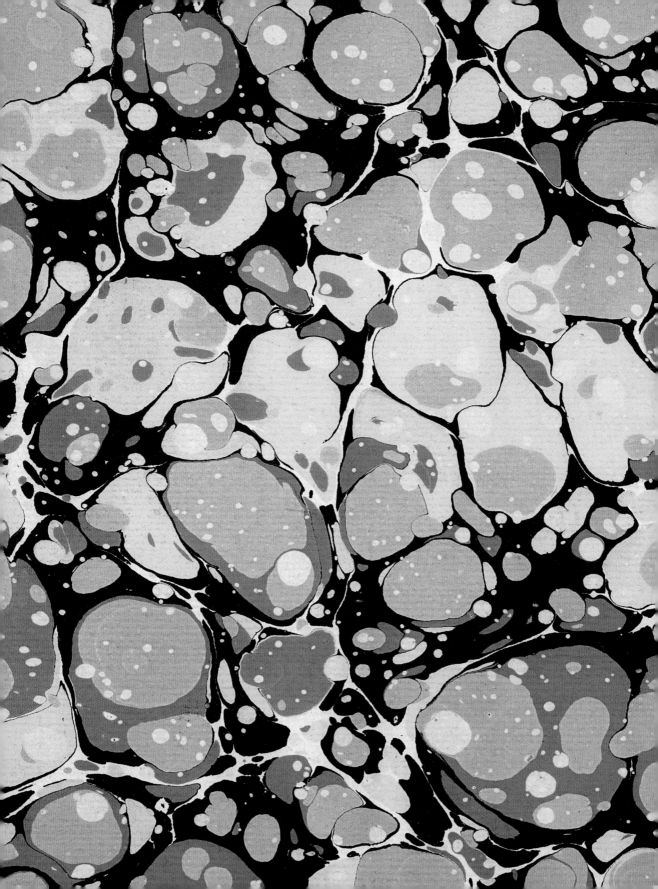

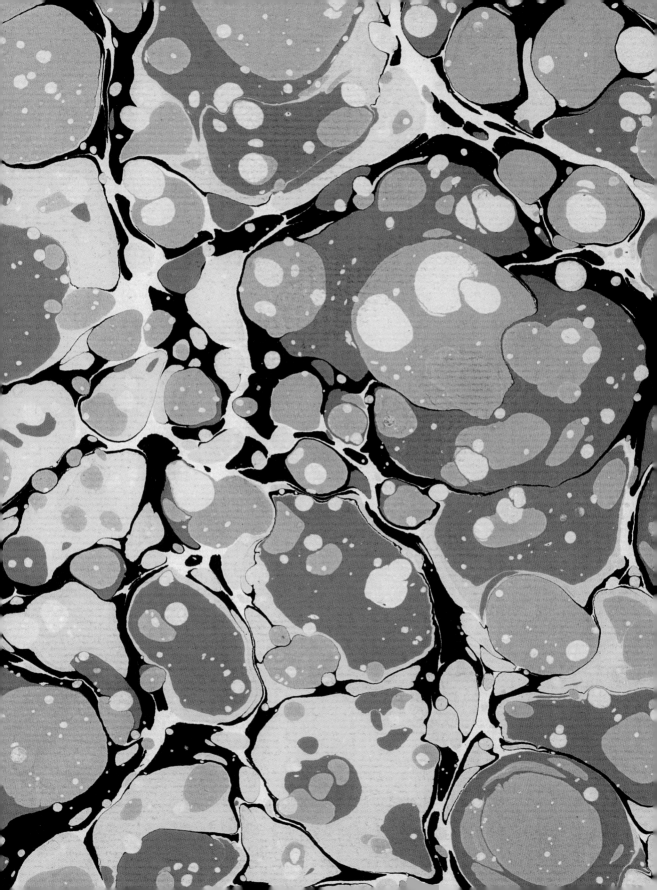

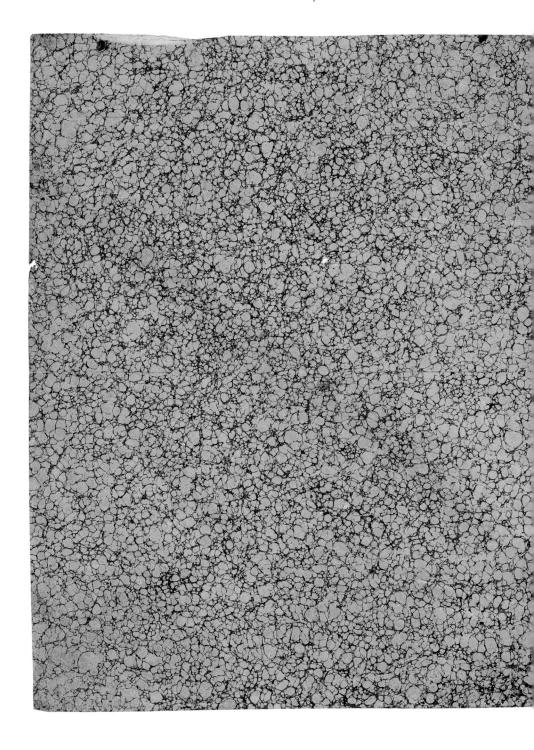

Pages 174–5
Nineteenth-century European
stone marbling (the oldest
style of marbling). J.1837

Above
Nineteenth-century European
vein marbling. J.1782

Austrian decorated paper made
by the Wiener Werkstätte (Vienna
Workshop) in 1910. Established
in 1903, the workshop brought
together artists and designers
of all disciplines in an attempt
to imbue functional objects with
an aesthetic appeal. J.2993.a

Opposite and above
Twentieth-century lithography by
the German artist Erich Büttner
(1889–1936). An active member of
the Berlin Secession, Büttner was
closely linked with the publishing
world, producing illustrations and
editing his own literary magazine.
J.2831, J.2832

Page 180
Nineteenth-century European
comb marbling. This style of
marbling was commonly used
for end-leaves. J.1895

Page 181
Nineteenth-century European
marbling. This form of decoration
was commonly used to cover books
or as end-leaves. J.1782.b

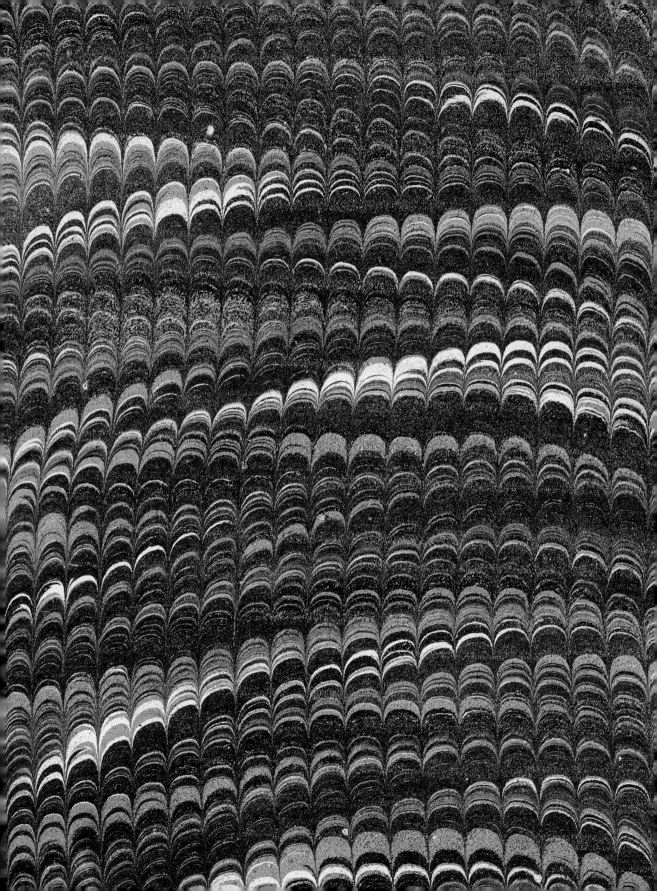

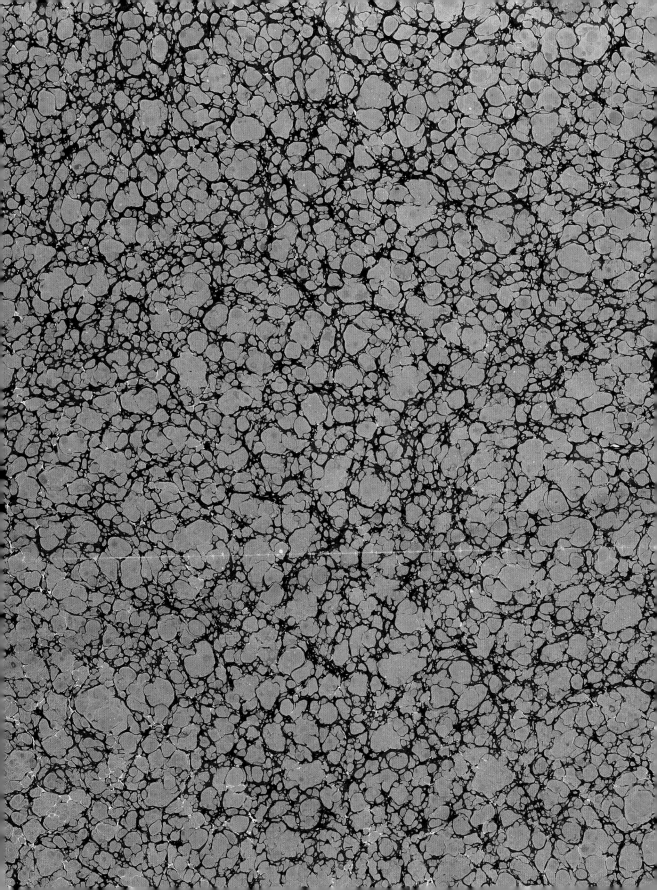

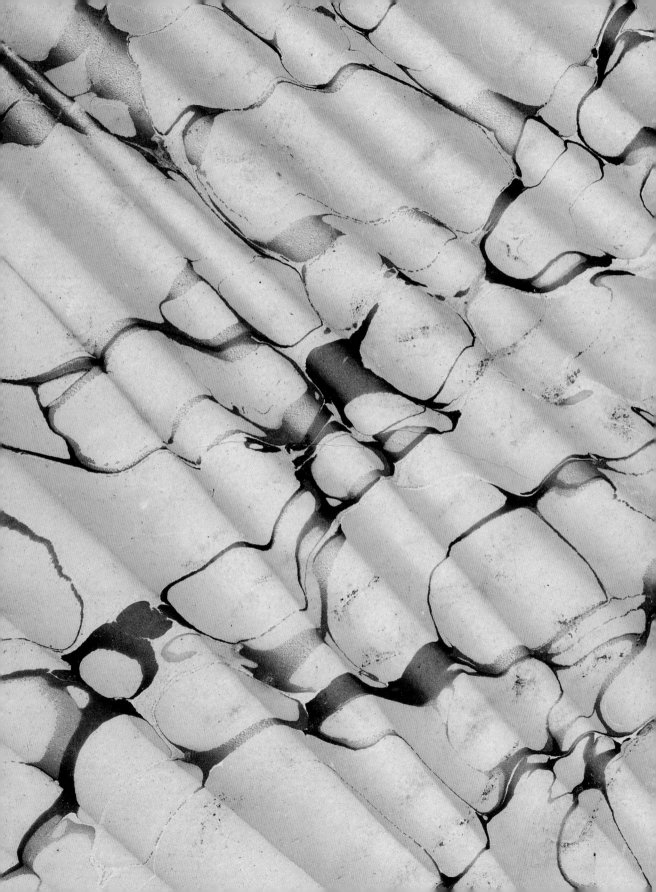

Page 182
Twentieth-century European
marbling. It seems likely that
the designer created the pattern
with the aid of an implement of
some kind, such as a stylus. J.1898

Page 183
An example of late nineteenth-
century European Spanish
marbling. J.1900

Above
Twentieth-century lithography
by Axel Salto (1889–1961).
Salto was a Danish ceramicist,
jeweller, and graphic and textile
designer. His work, such as this
pattern known as 'Palm Tree',
was inspired by botanical forms.
YV.1989.b.1137 no.43

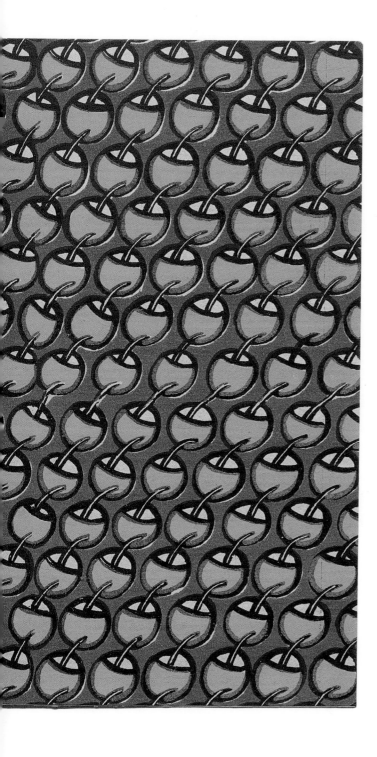

Twentieth-century lithography
by Axel Salto. As this pattern
called 'Fruits' demonstrates, Salto
was also inspired by art deco.
YV.1989.b.1137 no.32

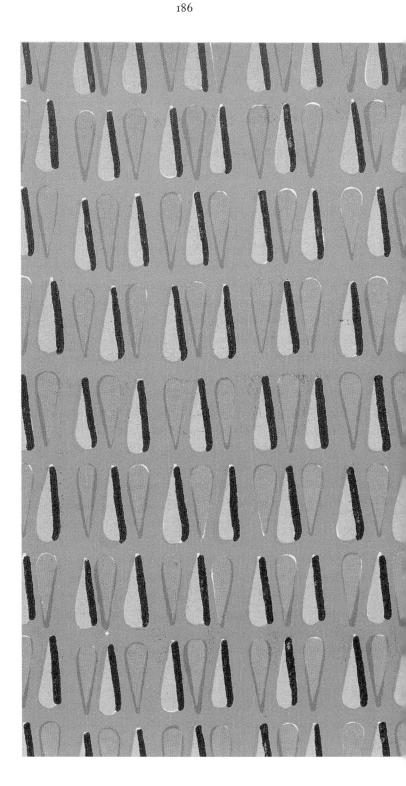

Twentieth-century lithography
by Axel Salto. Salto's textile and
paper designs had much in
common, including the techniques
used to produce them. This
colourful pattern was called 'Arabic'.
YV.1989.b.1137 no.20

Left
Twentieth-century lithography
by Axel Salto. This pattern,
called 'Parachute', is reminiscent
of Salto's ceramics, which were
rarely smooth and featured odd
protuberances. YV.1989.b.1137 no.8

Pages 188–9
Nineteenth-century European
Spanish marbling. Note the tension
between the strong diagonal lines
and the web of veining. J.1908

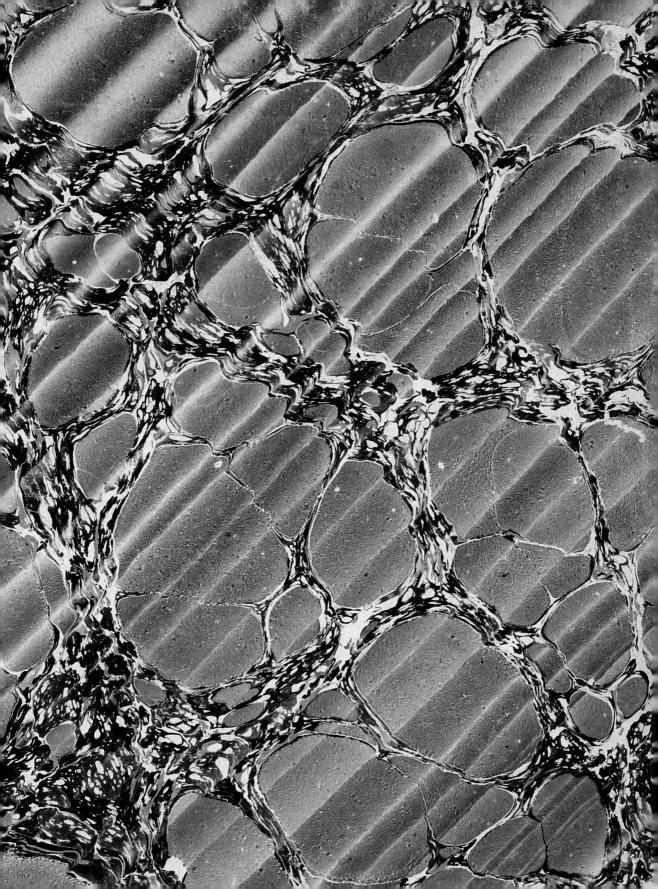

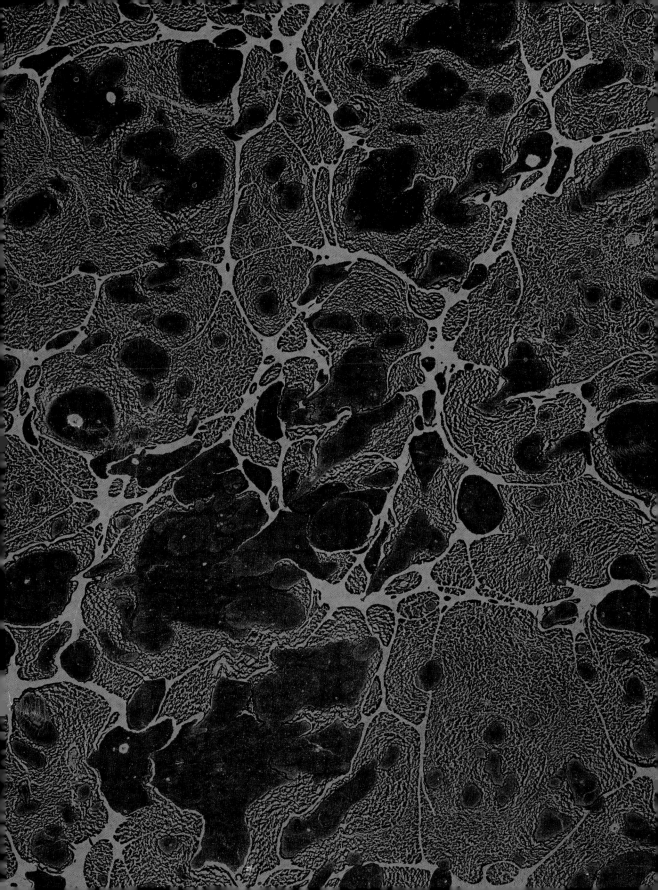

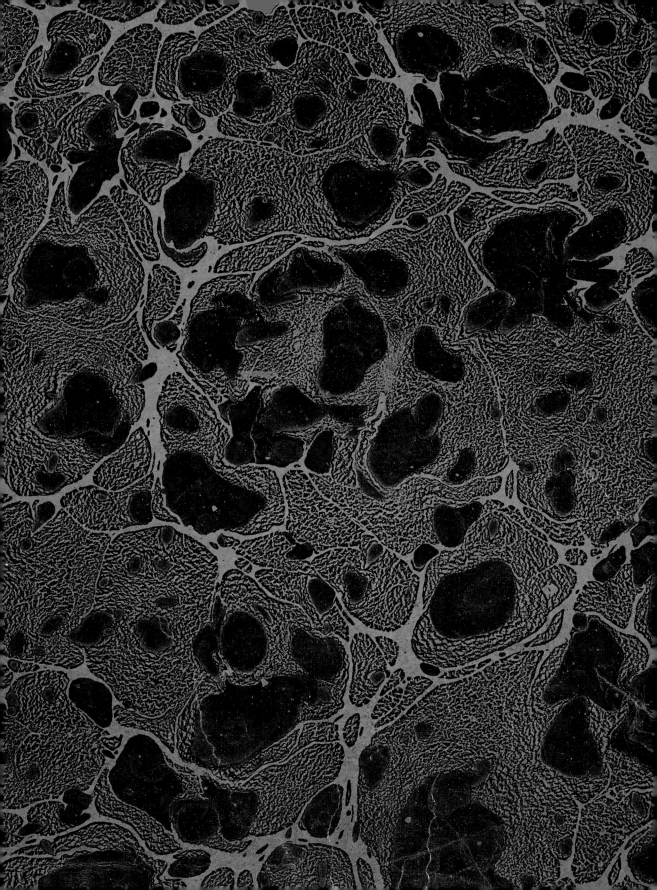

Pages 190–1
Nineteenth-century European
marbling, probably German. J.1862

This spread
Twentieth-century lithography
by Erich Büttner. The design
at bottom right was created for
the cover of Otto Ernst's novella
Himmel voller Geigen (A sky full
of violins; 1923), part of a series
of books bound by Büttner in
the 1920s for the Berlin-based
publishing house Mosaik-Bücher.
Büttner's work was noted for
its 'dark colourfulness'.
Clockwise from top left: J.2810,
J.2812, J.2811, J.2814

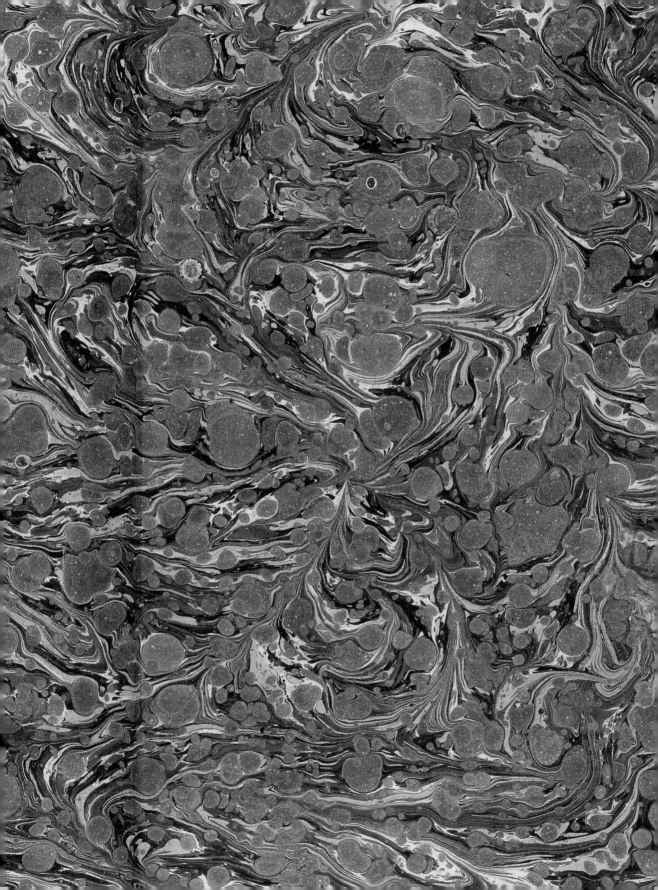

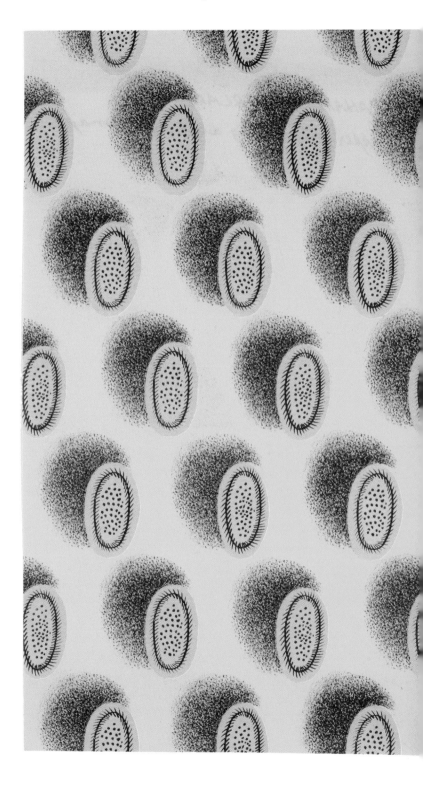

Page 194
Twentieth-century lithography
by John Woodcock (b. 1927), a
British map-maker, engraver and
dust-jacket designer employed by
the Curwen Press and Penguin
Books. J.2959

Page 195
Nineteenth-century European
stone marbling. J.1791.a

Right
Twentieth-century lithography
by the British artist Graham
Sutherland (1903–1980). From the
late 1940s, a number of influential
British artists became involved in
book design. Providing the original
artwork in the form of a copper
engraving, for example, they would
leave technicians to complete the
lithographic process. J.2940

Opposite
Nineteenth-century German
marbling by Paul Kersten (1899).
J.1936

Page 198
Late nineteenth-century European lithography (1870). This example demonstrates how the lithographic process was used to create detailed and colourful papers. J.2768.c

Page 199
Late nineteenth-century German marbling by Paul Kersten, made at the Aschaffenburger Buntpapierfabrik (decorated-paper factory) in 1899. J.1939

Page 200
Nineteenth-century European moiré marbling incorporating veining in gold (the latter may have been added via a lithographic process). J.1935

Page 201
Twentieth-century lithography by Erich Büttner. This design was for a book cover and end-leaves. J.2833

Page 202
Twentieth-century lithography by Erich Büttner. Büttner created this design for another title in the Mosaik-Bücher series (see page 193), Max Kretzer's *Die Locke* (1922). Kretzer was a fellow expressionist whose interests revolved around the conditions of the urban working classes. J.2818

Page 203
Nineteenth-century European marbling. This particular style of marbling is known as 'Stormont'. J.1779

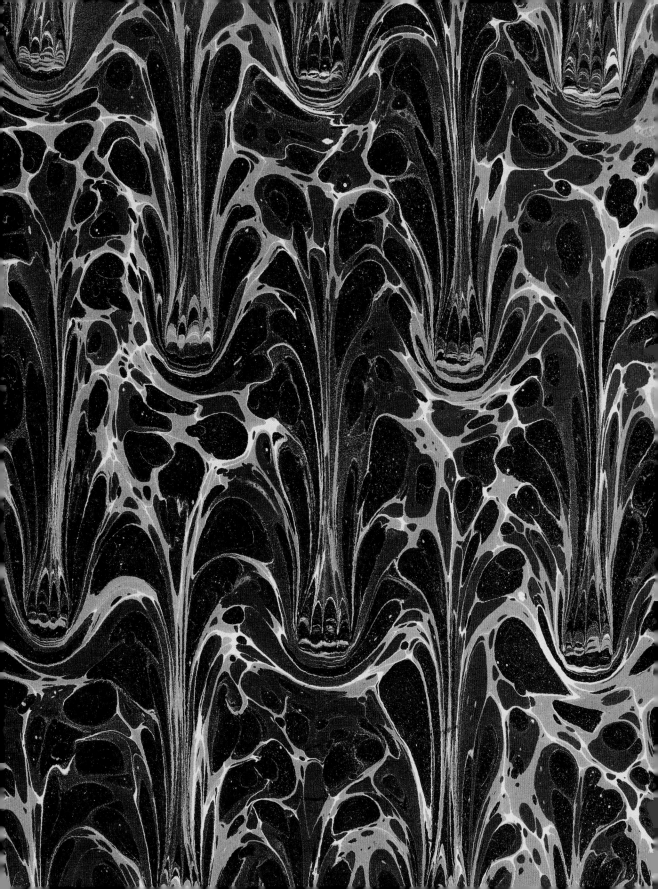

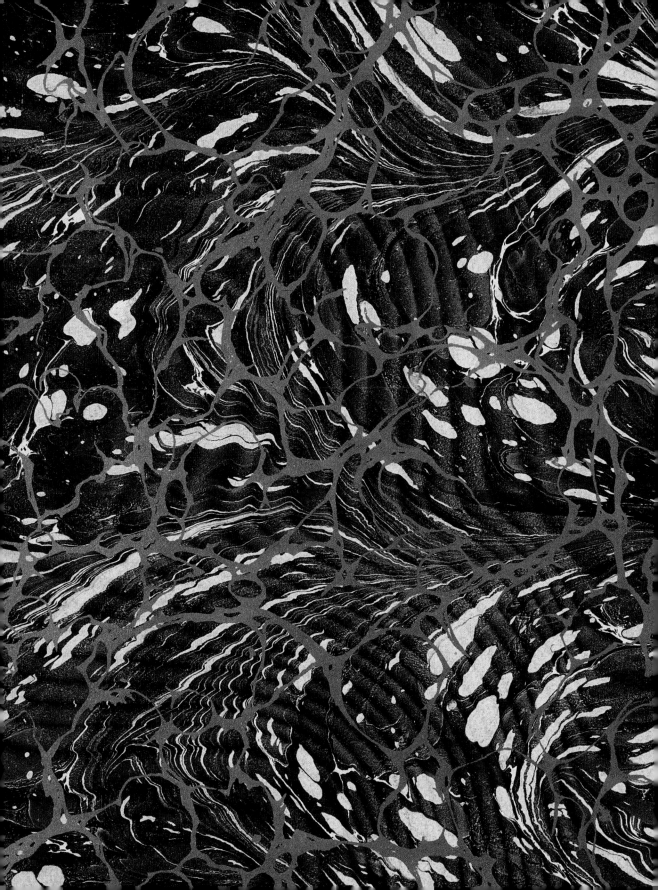

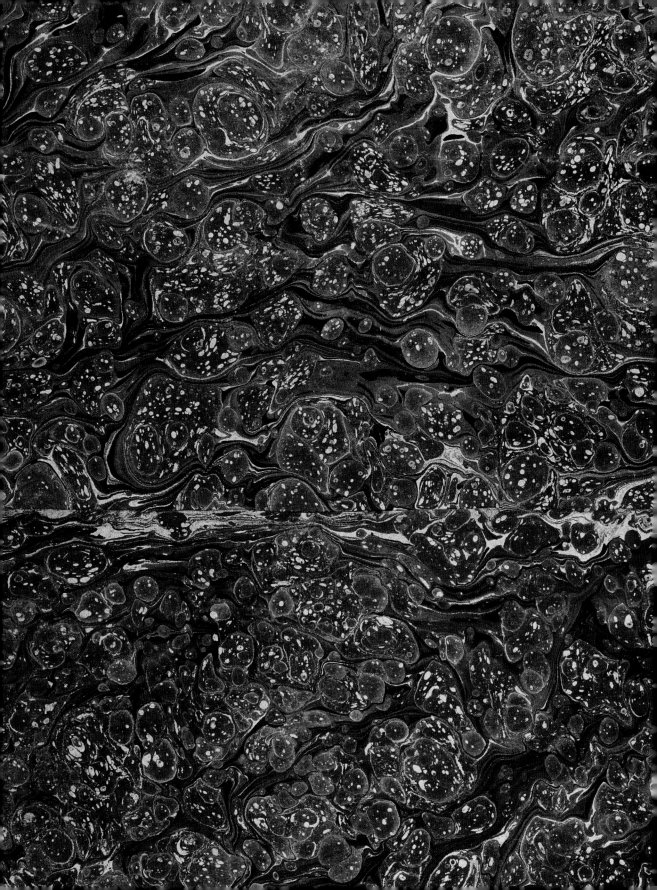

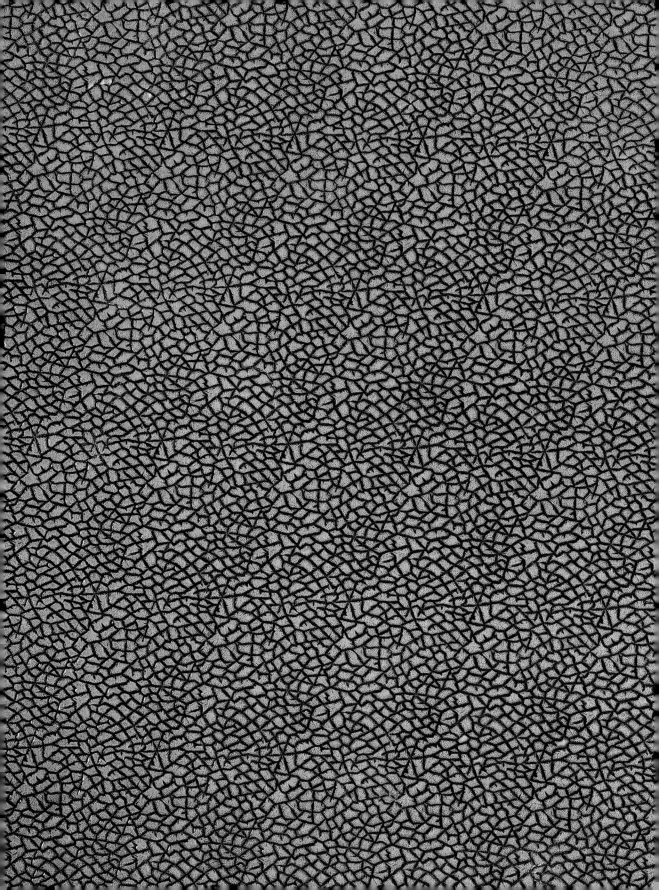

MISCELLANEOUS DECORATING TECHNIQUES

In addition to the techniques already discussed, there are many more ways in which to decorate paper, either by hand or mechanically. The principles often remain the same, whether using a handheld rubber roller or industrial-sized engraved cylinders. With the former, however, comes a certain irregularity and spontaneity, while the latter gives a much more exact result. Onlays are easily applied; inlays sometimes appear, but usually as part of the paper-*making* process, as, for example, when flower petals are added to the pulp. Other techniques include sprinkling, dribbling, crinkling and folding.

'Fancy papers' is a term often used rather imprecisely. Generally speaking, it is used to refer to printed patterned papers created for stationery (gift wrapping, writing paper, invitations, etc.) and packaging (including for food). It can also be used in a more general sense. Victorian manufacturers used the term to refer to a wide variety of decorated papers (see page 13), while Edward Seymour of the Fancy Paper Company of London (*c.* 1919–71) produced marbled papers.[1]

Fig. 1: Details of two nineteenth-century Italian flocked end-leaves. From *Ospizio degli Armeni in Roma, Ode tratta dall'Armeno*, Venice, 1834. B.27

Fig. 2: Silhouette paper from a copy of Jacob van der Heyden, *Speculum Cornelianum*, Strasbourg, 1618, used as an *album amicorum*. B.3 p.21

Flock papers

Flock paper (in existence in fifteenth-century Italy) was made by gluing coloured wool dust to the surface of the paper. Some techniques involved the application of glue using a block (as in block printing) or stencil. Flock wall hangings were particularly popular in England from the sixteenth to the eighteenth centuries, and in France in the eighteenth century. Flock papers were commonly used as wallpapers, but also, although rarely, as end-leaves (see fig. 1). Examples of historical flock papers are rare: the flock surfaces rubbed away and soon looked shabby, so the papers were discarded.

Silhouette papers

It is difficult to determine how silhouette papers were made since historical accounts of its production are few and unclear. According to some authorities, thin pieces of leather were cut into shapes, soaked in dye and pressed between two sheets of thin paper.[2] Richard J. Wolfe notes that another method may have resembled stencilling (see below).[3] Silhouette papers often formed part of an *album amicorum* (see fig. 2).

Stencilling

This versatile and labour-saving method involved the passing of colour through holes in a thin sheet of material, such as impregnated cardboard or sheeted zinc, in order to decorate the paper beneath (see fig. 3). Little training was needed (children were sometimes employed to produce stencilled paper), multiple copies of the same stencil could be cut at a single time (depending on the material) and the stencils could be reused.

Japanese stencil-making using layers of waterproof mulberry paper flourished from the 1600s. These stencils were used to apply motifs to textiles (the practice known as *katagami*; see page 16) as well as paper. A more sophisticated method of stencilling may have been used for the decorative margins of Near Eastern albums and manuscripts, such as the illuminated manuscript *Khamsa of Nizami* made for the Mughal emperor Akbar in the early 1590s (see fig. 6).[4]

Batik papers

The wax-resist method used in batik was probably first employed in ancient Egypt for the decoration of cloth. Use later spread to China and Japan, but it is most often associated with Indonesia. The technique involves the application of a base colour followed by a design in wax, then another colour, and so on. Eventually, the wax is melted away to reveal layers of colour. In the 1940s the Swiss bookbinder and teacher Emil Kretz (1896–1960) developed a technique he called 'paste' or 'roller batik', using paste instead of wax and oil paints as colourants (see fig. 5).[5]

Fig. 3: Sixteenth-century woodcut by Jost Amman of a German craftsman using a stencil. From *Eigentliche Beschreibung Aller Stande auff Erden*, Frankfurt, 1568.

Fig. 4: Sixteenth-century Mughal paper decorated by means of several techniques (see also fig. 6). Or.12208

Fig. 5: Twentieth-century batik paper by Emil Kretz. J.3616

Combined techniques

In common with artistic styles, paper-decorating techniques do not have to be used one at a time. As paper-decorators from both East (see figs 4 and 6) and West have shown (and, indeed, continue to show), a stunning overall effect can be achieved by combining more than one approach.

Historically, coloured backgrounds were frequently scattered with small pieces of gold or silver leaf, or with powdered mica (a mineral). Even paper completely covered with gold was sometimes adorned, as indicated by J. Ovington in his account of his visit to the Indian state of Gujarat in the late seventeenth century. In contrast to the paper 'which is of ordinary use', he wrote, 'that which they write upon, either to the emperor or persons of consequence, is gilt all on the surface, as ours is on the edges with some small flowers interspersed here and there for ornaments'.[6]

Since the early nineteenth century and the advent of industrial, photographic and digital processes, many new methods and combinations of techniques have evolved.[7] Add to this the inventiveness and inspiration of countless practitioners, and it would seem that, today, there are as many combinations and methods as there are paper decorators.

Fig. 6: Calligraphy with decorated border, from the sixteenth-century
illustrated manuscript *Khamsa of Nizami*. The enlarged bird motifs (right)
suggest the initial use of a stencil with freehand additions. Or.12208

Above
Nineteenth-century block printing
covering a copy of *Das Denkmal
zu Reisbach im Vilsthale von
Niederbayern* (1845) by Karl
Lautenbacher. Its good condition
demonstrates the enduring quality
of such decorated paper. B.65

Pages 210 and 211
Nineteenth- to twentieth-century
European papers, probably printed
using lithography (which was
a relatively cheap process).
J.3168, J.3112

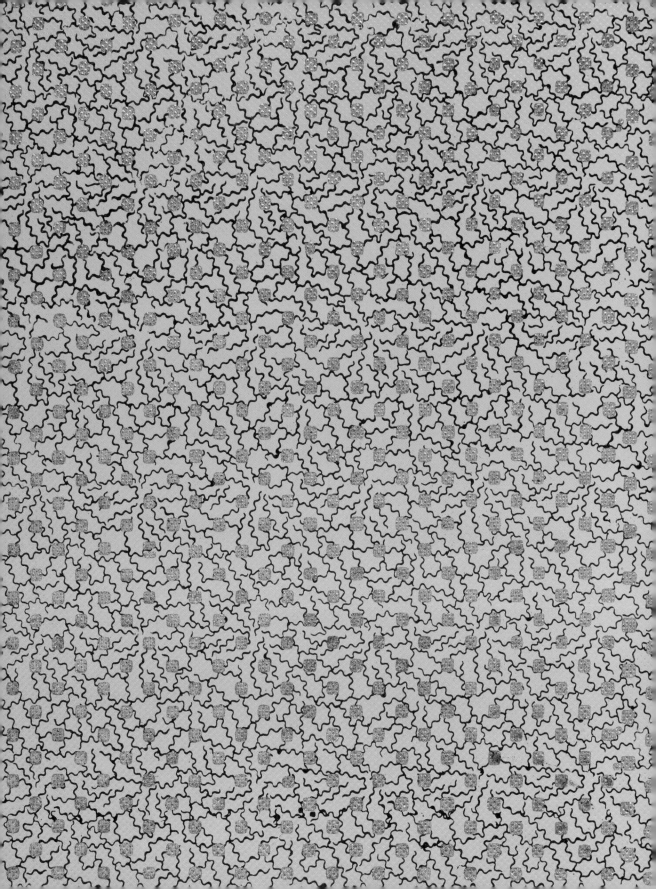

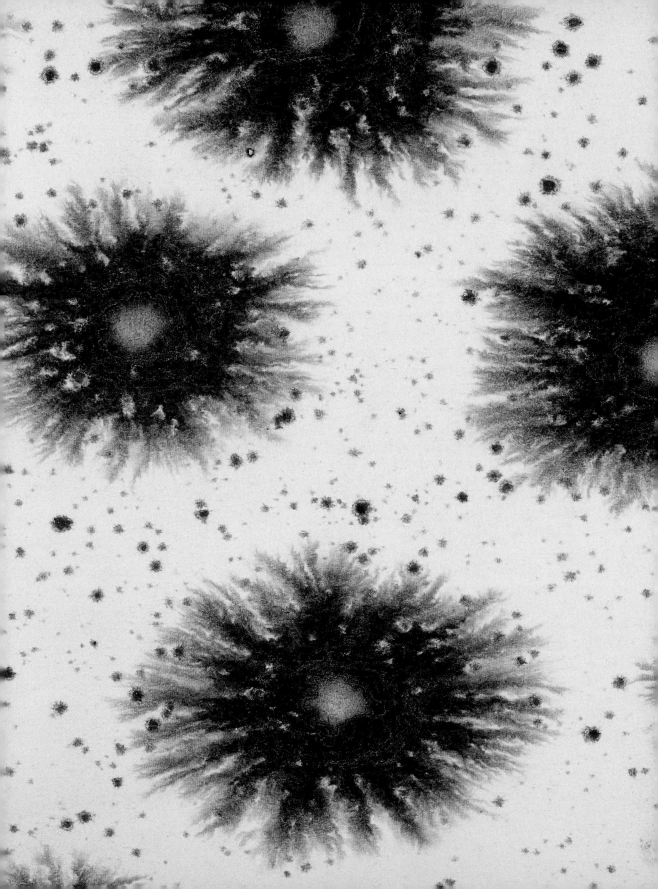

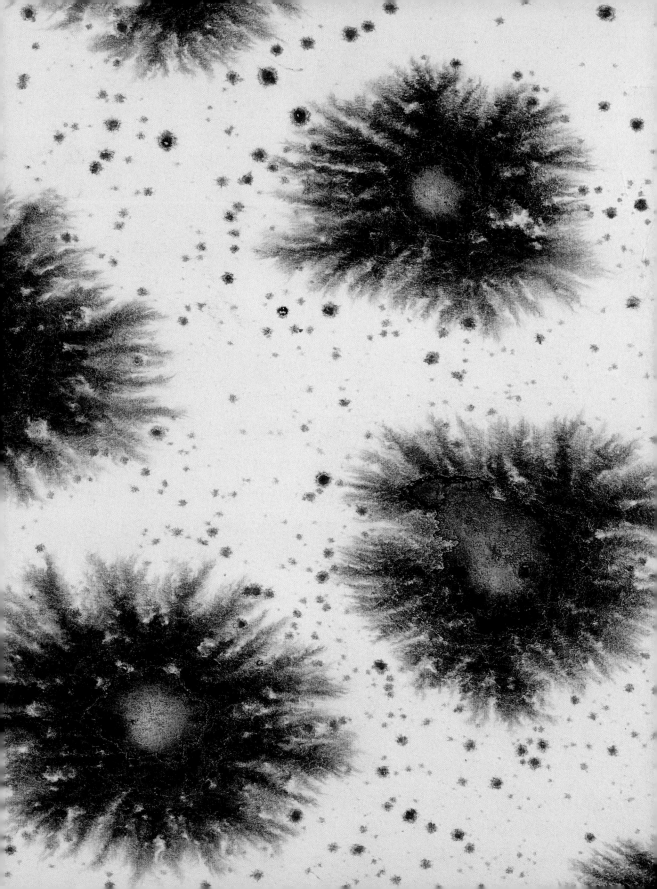

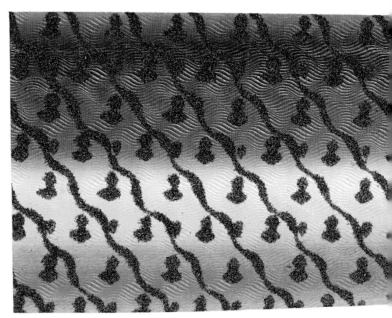

Pages 212–13
Twentieth-century German
paper by Paul Kersten (1905).
The exact technique used is difficult
to determine. Paints have been
sprinkled and dropped on to
the surface, and the addition of
chemicals also seems likely. J.2559

This spread
Nineteenth- to twentieth-century
European flocking and stencilling.
Clockwise from top left: J.1457,
J.1458, J.1459, J.1455

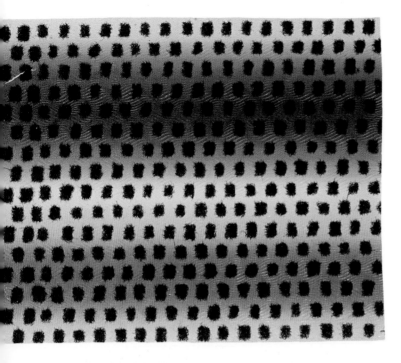

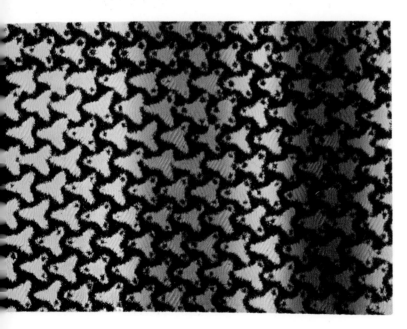

Pages 216 and 217
Nineteenth-century European
papers. Olga Hirsch detected the
use of either roller printing (similar
to block printing but with, say, an
engraved cylinder) or lithography.
Silk-screen printing could also be
considered; indeed, this may explain
the thickness of the paint.
J.3107, J.3212

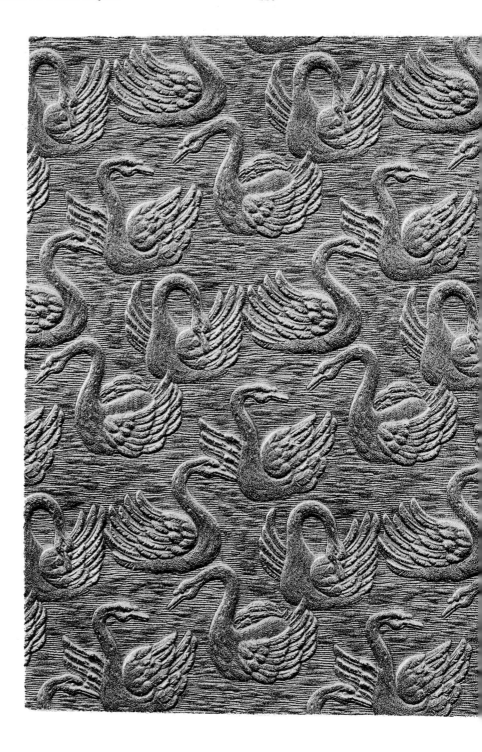

Page 218
Twentieth-century European
paper. A combination of techniques
was employed to produce this
design, including sprinkling, the use
of a stylus or other utensil, and the
application of chemicals. J.2702

Page 219
Twentieth-century German
stencilling (*c.* 1920) by Annemarie
Irmler, a skilled proponent of
the technique. J.3000.k

Page 222
Twentieth-century (1904)
printing using heat by Otto Hupp
(1859–1949), a German graphic
designer and heraldry specialist.
Metallic papers were prized
for the impression of opulence
they provided; the art nouveau
movement particularly favoured
gold. Thanks to nineteenth-century
advances in printing, such papers
could be produced economically
and in bulk. J.3107

Page 223
Twentieth-century stencilling by
Paul Kersten. In the hands of those
who were open to experimentation,
such technological innovations
as the airbrush, as used here
by Kertsen, had a major impact
on paper decoration. J.2701

Above
Probably twentieth-century
European embossing. This process
was used to apply surface texture
to papers. Here, the swan motifs
are raised above the surface. J.3108

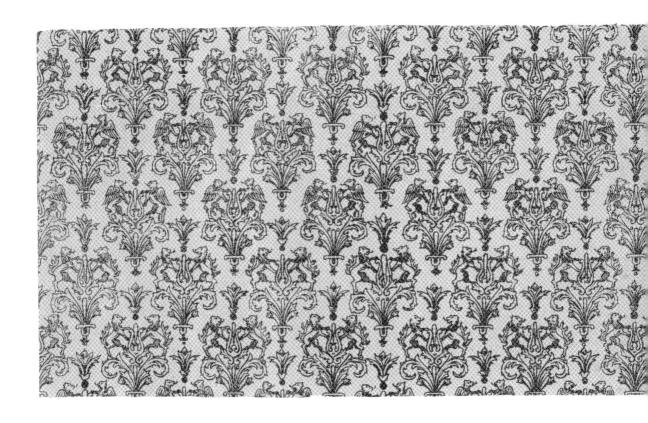

Page 224
Twentieth-century European
lithography. The pattern consists
of horizontal rows of black dots
overlaid with gold-coloured
floating petals. J.3210

Page 225
Twentieth-century European
lithography. Note how the
horizontal hatching helps to give
the flat sheet a three-dimensional
appearance. J.3206.a

Above
Twentieth-century European
embossing and lithography.
The invention of continuous
rolls of paper made paper
decoration quicker and easier.
A close inspection of the pattern
seen here reveals the heraldic form
of two lions rampant. J.3207.a

Opposite
Nineteenth-century European
embossing. Here, the pale-coloured
motif stands considerably proud
of the orange paper surface. J.3073

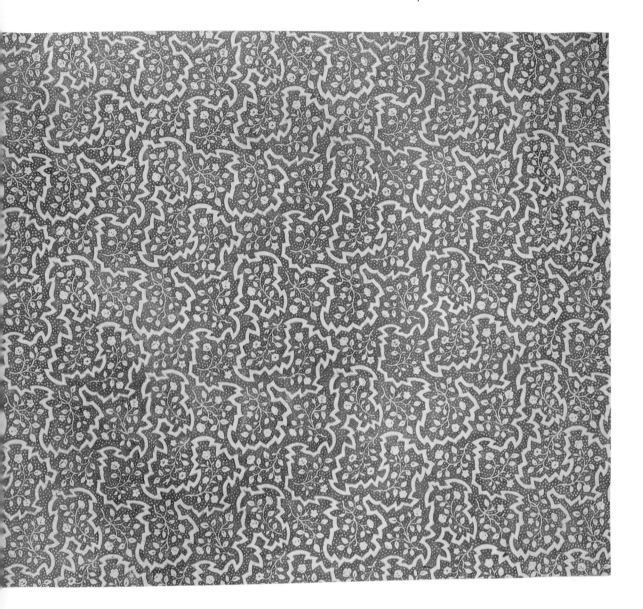

Page 228
Twentieth-century European decoration, a combination of several transfer methods (e.g. block printing or lithography). Without reference to the maker's instructions and a high level of magnification, it can be difficult to determine exactly which of the more modern techniques have been used. J.3174

Page 229
Early twentieth-century lithography by Johann Vincenz Cissarz (1873–1942). Cissarz was active in the Dresden craft workshops, particularly in the area of commercial art. He also taught, although his efforts did not always meet with success. One of his students, the Austrian painter Marie-Louise von Motesiczky, considered him 'a chattering, dogmatic, skilful and good-natured idiot'. J.3294

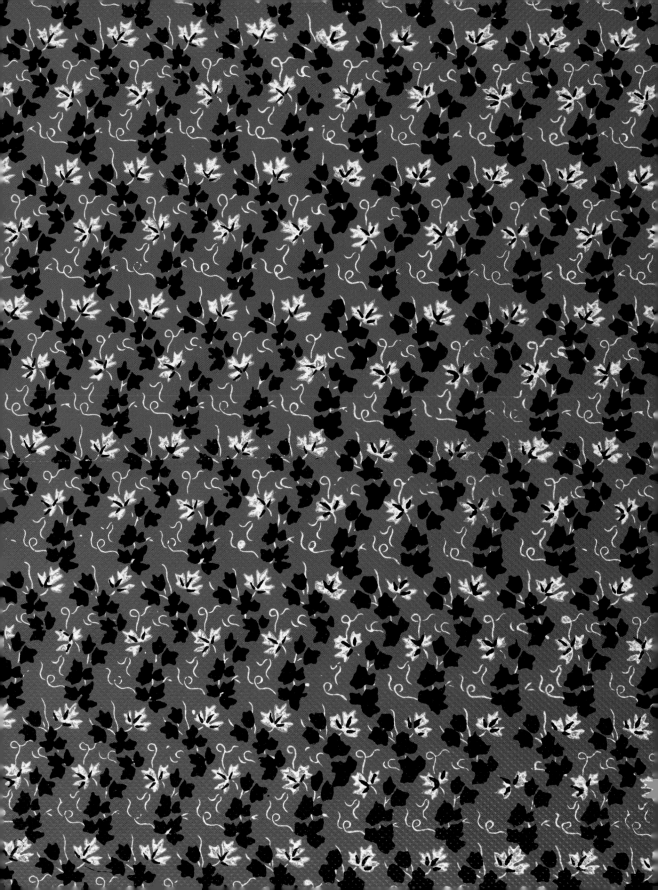

Pages 230 and 231
Twentieth-century European
papers, probably created using
lithography. The example on page
230 demonstrates the effectiveness
of simple, bold designs, especially
the use of contrasting colours.
The example on the opposite page
is more delicate, with the gold-
coloured spots and thin, wavy
lines imparting a sense of
movement. J.3171, J.3172

Above and opposite
Twentieth-century lithography by
Johann Vincent Cissarz. Cissarz
was noted for his work in the field
of book arts. His cover designs, for
example, reflected the text within,
a practice increasingly common
from the early twentieth century.
J.3292, J.3290

Pages 234 and 235
Probably twentieth-century European decoration featuring lithography. In common with early block printing by hand, this more recent technique could produce continuous patterns that successfully covered the whole surface, often by means of spots and hatching. The examples shown here may be technically perfect, however, but they appear rather flat and lack the energy associated with manual, less accurate printing methods. J.3194, J.3192.a

Twentieth-century lithography by
Johann Vincent Cissarz. The art
nouveau movement (*Jugendstil* in
German) encouraged interest in
the portrayal of nature, particularly
flowers. J.3293

Left
Seventeenth-century German
marbling and stencilling (using
a variety of different shapes). Paper
decorators used innovation as a
means of increasing sales. In the
case of the *album amicorum*, the
use of marbled shapes, including
architectural motifs and heraldic
shields, on each page was one way
of catching the eye of potential
purchasers. B.3

Page 238
Nineteenth-century German
lithography (*c.* 1890). In the
lithographic process, the plates
used for transferring the image
to the paper can be made from
a variety of materials. Initially,
smooth stones were used, but
experiments saw the introduction
of more modern materials.
According to a note by Olga
Hirsch, this floral example
was printed from a lead plate.
J.3213.a

Page 239
Nineteenth-century European
decoration embracing several
transfer methods. Such details
as the horizontal hatching and
the 'fish scales' beneath the urns
indicate the versatility of these
methods, successfully conveying
both light and dark. J.3213.b

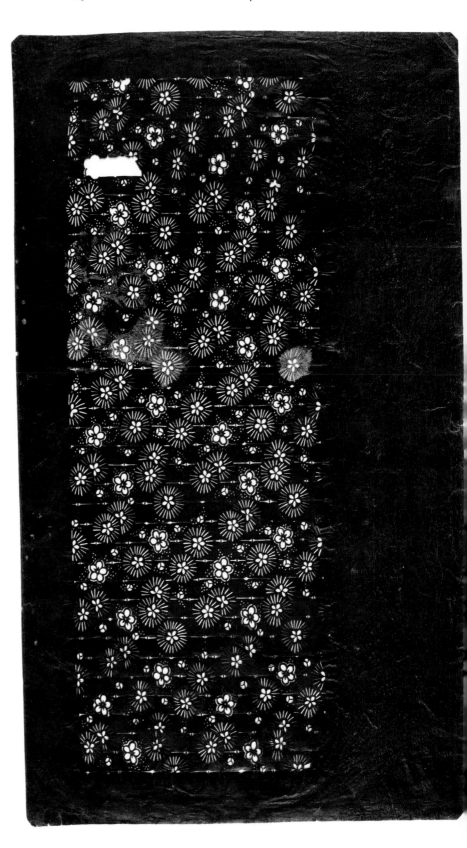

Right and opposite
Two examples of nineteenth-
to twentieth-century *katagami*.
Mulberry paper was used because
it was durable and did not fray
when cut. J.3562, J.3560

Pages 242–3
Probably late nineteenth-
century European printing with
lithography. Note the chinoiserie
details. J.3211

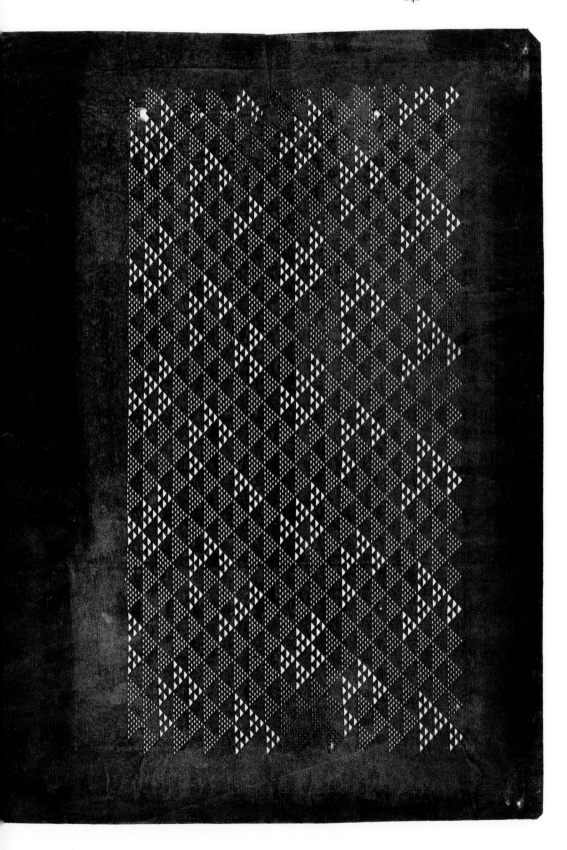

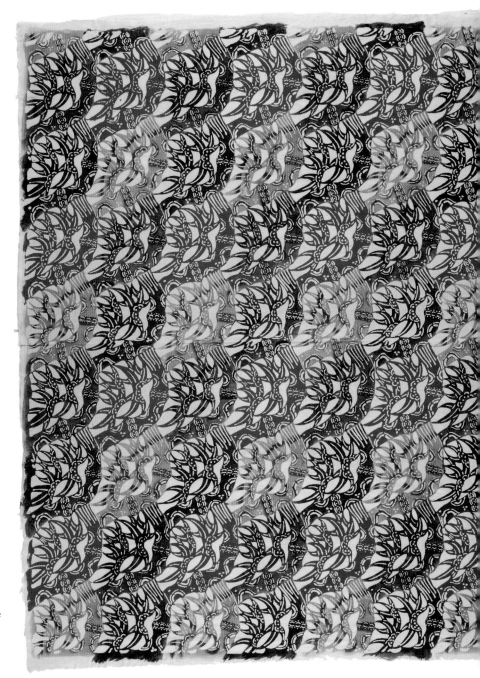

Page 244
Probably twentieth-century
European embossing. At the
heart of the design is a repeating
bird motif. J.3209

Page 245
Probably late nineteenth-century
Chinese floral pattern on a
background of red, a colour
considered lucky in Chinese
culture. In terms of texture and
thickness, the paper is noticeably
different from that used in the
West. Chinese papers varied in
their composition depending on
which raw materials were most
readily available at the time.
Different sizes and surfaces
were also used. J.3563

Right
Twentieth-century example
of *katazome*, a Japanese form
of stencilling that uses paste to
resist the colouring agent. It was
commonly used to dye textiles,
but here has been used to decorate
paper. Of this particular design,
Olga Hirsch suggested that it
owed much to *bingata*, a historic
textile-decorating technique
from Okinawa. J.3566.b

Opposite
Nineteenth-century Far Eastern
paper featuring white fibres. The
cloudy appearance prized in many
decorated papers may be achieved
by a variety of methods. Some,
such as the incorporation of
material into the pulp, are part of
the paper-making rather than the
paper-decorating process. J.3565

Page 248
Nineteenth-century European
embossing. J.3207

Page 249
Nineteenth- to twentieth-century
Far Eastern paper in imitation
of embossed leather. (The style
was also in use in Europe.) Note
the caged-bird motif. J.3564

NOTES

INTRODUCTION

1. In Spain, most decorated papers are of the marbled variety; see http://marblinginspain. blogspot.de (accessed June 2015). For information on decorated papers in the Netherlands, see www.kb.nl/en/themes/ book-art-and-illustrated-books/decorated-paper (accessed July 2015).

2. See André Jammes, *Papiers dominotés: trait d'union entre l'imagerie populaire et les papiers peints (France, 1750–1820)*, Paris, 2010, p. 9.

3. Susanne Krause (ed.), *Buntpapier: ein Bestimmungsbuch/Decorated Paper: A Guide Book/Sierpapier: een gids*, Hamburg, 2009, p. 140.

4. This account was recorded by the historian Fan Hua (398–445) in his biography of Cai Lun. The origins of paper are discussed in Józef Dabrowski, 'Remarks on the Invention of True Paper by Cai Lun', in *Institute of Paper History Congress Book*, vol. 16, 2006, pp. 5–15.

5. Several dates have been suggested, from 1–2 BC, during the Western Han dynasty, to as early as 8 BC. See Dabrowski, 'Remarks'. The International Dunhuang Project has information on early paper. See http://idp.bl.uk/pages/conservation_specialisms.a4d (accessed June 2015).

6. Richard J. Wolfe, *Marbled Paper: Its History, Techniques, and Patterns*, Philadelphia, 1990, p. 5.

7. See *ibid.*, p. 6, and Joseph Needham (ed.), *Science and Civilisation in China*, vol. 5, part 1, *Paper and Printing* by Tsien Tsuen-Hsuin, Cambridge, 1985, pp. 87–96.

8. Barry McKay, *Patterns and Pigments in English Marbled Papers: An Account of the Origins, Sources and Documentary Literature to 1881*, Kidlington, 1988, p. 131.

9. Peter Kornicki, *The Book in Japan: A Cultural History from the Beginnings to the Nineteenth Century*, Hawaii, 2004, p. 41.

10. *Ibid.*, p. 42. Examples of Mitsuhiro's work can be seen online at www.scholten-japanese-art.com/sutras_04.htm and www.harvardartmuseums.org (accessed June 2015).

11. Rebecca Salter, *Japanese Popular Prints: From Votive Slips to Playing Cards*, London, 2006, p. 193.

12. McKay, *Patterns and Pigments*, p. 30.

13. An American work, *The Mysterious Marbler* by James Sumner, soon followed in 1854. There had also been previous examinations of the craft in Europe. See Wolfe, *Marbled Paper*, pp. 15–17 and a discussion of the Woolnough family on p. 79.

14. Tanya Schmoller, *Remondini and Rizzi: A Chapter in Italian Decorated Paper History*, New Castle, Del., 1990, p. 7.

15. Olga Hirsch Collection of Decorated Papers, Box 30 (J.2715–J.2796), Lithography: Industrial, British Library, London.

16. Curtis Evarts, 'A Européenerie Zitan Armchair', www.sothebys.com/it/auctions/2014/fine-chinese-ceramics-works-of-art-n09116/Fine-Chinese-Works-Art-Featured-Content/2014/02/a-europenerie-zitan.html (accessed June 2015).

17. Farley Grubb, 'Benjamin Franklin and the Birth of a Paper Money Economy', www.philadelphiafed.org/publications/economic-education/ben-franklin-and-paper-money-economy.pdf (accessed June 2015).

18. Tanya Schmoller, *To Brighten Things Up: The Schmoller Collection of Decorated Papers*, Manchester, 2008, p. 12.

19. *London Gazette*, 31 January 1854, p. 304, available online at www.thegazette.co.uk/London/issue/21517/page/304 (accessed June 2015).

20. *Pall Mall Gazette*, 12 August 1869, pp. 8–9. Many families would have lived on just a few shillings a week.

21. See theottomans.org/english/art_culture/ebru_2.asp and turkishculture.org/traditional-arts/marbling-113.htm (accessed June 2015).

22. Martin Luther, quoted in A. Hyatt Mayor, *Prints and People: A Social History of Printed Pictures*, New York, 1971, np (see under 'Holy Pictures').

23. Susan Dackerman, *Painted Prints: The Revelation of Color in Northern Renaissance & Baroque Engravings, Etchings and Woodcuts* (exh. cat.), Baltimore Museum of Art/Saint Louis Museum of Art, 2002–03, p. 30.

24. Thomas Bewick, quoted in Tessa Watt, *Cheap Print and Popular Piety, 1550–1640*, Cambridge, 1991, p. 167.

25. Goethe, *Aus meinem Leben: Dichtung und Wahrheit*, 1811–33, quoted in Christiane F. Kopylov, *Papiers dorés d'Allemagne au siècle des Lumières: suivis de quelques autres papiers décorés (Bilderbogen, Kattunpapiere & Herrnhutpapiere), 1680–1830*, Paris, 2012, p. 11.

26. *Cambridge Independent Press*, 3 April 1841, p. 4, and *Pall Mall Gazette*, 21 June 1888, p. 13.

27. One producer of such papers is Rossi 1931, based in Borgo San Lorenzo near Florence. See www.rossi1931.com.

28. Annabel Teh Gallop with Bernard Arps, *Golden Letters: Writing Traditions of Indonesia*, London, 1991, pp. 33–50.

29. *A Catalogue of the Harleian Manuscripts in the British Museum*, 4 vols, London, 1808–12, vol. 3, no. 6986, item 20.

30. Mirjam M. Foot, *Studies in the History of Bookbinding*, Aldershot, 1993, p. 288.

31. John Evelyn, 'An Exact Account of the Making of Marbled Paper', Royal Society, London, Classified Papers III (1), item 4.

32. I am grateful to Susanne Krause for this observation.

33. Catherine Hoover Voorsanger and John K. Howat (eds), *Art and the Empire City: New York, 1825–1861* (exh. cat.), Metropolitan Museum of Art, New York, 2000–01, p. 275.

34. Manfred Sellink, review of Dackerman, *Painted Prints*, in *Simiolus: Netherlands Quarterly for the History of Art*, vol. 30, no. 3/4, 2003, p. 253, available online at www.jstor.org/stable/3780919 (accessed June 2015).

35. Dackerman, *Painted Prints*, pp. 24–6.

36. *Ibid.*, p. 44.

37. Susanne Krause, *Mehr Kleisterpapier/More About Paste Paper*, Hamburg, 2005, p. 74.

38. Mehmet seems to have died by 1608, as implied in *Tertib-i Risale-i Ebri* (Organized Treatise on Marbling, 1608), the earliest known document on the practice of marbling. See Wolfe, *Marbled Paper*, p. 9, and www.ebruartusa.us/history.html (accessed June 2015). The Iranian/Persian term for marbling is 'abri'.

39. Examples of Miura's work can be seen at www.tinimiurabookbinding.com/Special%20Commissions.htm (accessed June 2015).

40. Isaiah Berlin (1909–1997) was a British philosopher, historian and social and political theorist. Quoted in Henry Hardy and Roger Hausheer (eds), *The Proper Study of Mankind: An Anthology of Essays*, London, 1997, p. 129.

41. See, for example, Benoît B. Mandelbrot, *Fractals: Form, Chance and Dimension*, San Francisco, 1977.

42. McKay, *Patterns and Pigments*, pp. 45–6.

HAND-MARBLED PAPERS

1. Barry McKay, *Patterns and Pigments in English Marbled Papers: An Account of the Origins, Sources and Documentary Literature to 1881*, Kidlington, 1988, p. 12. Some Turkish papers require a coating of the chemical compound alum to ensure the image adheres.

2. Olga Hirsch Collection of Decorated Papers, Box 43 (J.3526.a), Japan, China, Persia (or Turkish): Various Techniques, British Library, London. Box 43 contains a variety of this style of paper.

3. Historically, French authorities attributed the invention of marbling to several sources, including the seventeenth-century French binder Macé Ruette, and Diderot and d'Alembert's *Encyclopédie* (1751–72).

4. Thomas Levenson, *Newton and the Counterfeiter: The Unknown Detective Career of the World's Greatest Scientist*, London, 2009, p. 134.

5. Diana Patterson, 'John Baskerville, Marbler', *Library*, vol. s6-12, no. 3, 1990, p. 215.

6. Mirjam Foot, 'The Olga Hirsch Collection of Decorated Papers', *British Library Journal*, vol. 7, no. 1, Spring 1981, p. 25.

7. For illustrated examples of the different styles, see Susanne Krause (ed.), *Buntpapier: ein Bestimmungsbuch/Decorated Paper: A Guide Book/Sierpapier: een gids*, Hamburg, 2009.

8. See Richard J. Wolfe, *Marbled Paper: Its History, Techniques, and Patterns*, Philadelphia, 1990, p. 125.

9. Silvanus P. Thompson, *Michael Faraday: His Life and Work*, London, 1898, p. 249.

10. Taken from Ernst-Peter Biesalski, 'Die Entwicklung der industriellen Buchbinderei im 19. Jahrhundert', in Dag-Ernst Petersen, *Gebunden in der Dampfbuchbinderei: Buchbinden im Wandel des 19. Jahrhunderts*, Wiesbaden, 1994, p. 82. Originally published in Paul Adam, *Systematisches Lehr- und Handbuch der Buchbinderei*, supplement, Dresden, 1891. It is not clear exactly how the device would have worked, if indeed it worked at all. It may have been more suitable for the decoration of walls.

PASTE PAPERS

1. Susanne Krause, *Paste Paper/Kleisterpapier*, trans. Susanne Krause and Claire Bolton, Marcham, 2002, p. 16.

2. I am indebted to Susanne Krause for this information.

3. Claire Bolton, *Maziarczyk Paste Papers*, Oxford, 1991, pp. 3–4.

4. James H. Fraser, *The Paste Papers of the Golden Hind Press*, Madison, NJ, 1983, p. 8.

BROCADE PAPERS

1. Mirjam Foot, 'The Olga Hirsch Collection of Decorated Papers', *British Library Journal*, vol. 7, no. 1, Spring 1981, p. 28. An imperial privilege was an official licence issued on behalf of the Holy Roman Emperor without which certain types of decorated paper could not be made. Stoy (1670–1750) was a major producer of many types of decorated paper in Augsburg.

2. *Ibid.*, p. 34.

3. Part of a series called 'Bibliothèque de la jeunesse chrétienne'.

BLOCK-PRINTED PAPERS

1. André Jammes, *Papiers dominotés: trait d'union entre l'imagerie populaire et les papiers peints (France, 1750–1820)*, Paris, 2010, p. 27.

2. Ann Herring, *The World of Chiyogami: Hand-Printed Patterned Papers of Japan*, Tokyo/New York, 1987, pp. 8–9.

3. *Ibid.*, p. 26.

MASS PRODUCTION
The Nineteenth Century and Beyond

1. 'Lithography', www.britannica.com/topic/lithography (accessed June 2015).

2. Sue Allen, 'Floral-Patterned Endpapers in Nineteenth-Century American Books', *Winterthur Portfolio*, vol. 12, 1977, p. 197.

3. See Olga Hirsch Collection of Decorated Papers, Folder 32 (J.2852–J.2960), Lithography: British Artists (late 1940s – early 1960s), British Library, London. The papers of the Curwen Press are now held by Cambridge University Library; see MS Add.9853/C1.

4. Stanley Morison, quoted in Tanya Schmoller, *Remondini and Rizzi: A Chapter in Italian Decorated Paper History*, New Castle, Del., 1990, p. 7.

5. Curwen Press, *A Specimen Book of Pattern Papers Designed for and in use at the Curwen Press*, intro. Paul Nash, London, 1928, p. xii.

MISCELLANEOUS DECORATING TECHNIQUES

1. Sidney E. Berger, *Edward Seymour and the Fancy Paper Company: The Story of a British Marbled Paper Manufacturer*, New Castle, Del., 2006. The Olga Hirsch collection has several examples of Seymour's marbling. See Box 22 (J.1981–J.2044), Marbling: 20th Century Artists' Papers, J.2002–J.2012: Trough marbles by Mr E. Seymour, London, with ms notes describing the techniques used, British Library, London.

2. Albert Haemmerle, *Buntpapier: Herkommen, Geschichte, Techniken, Beziehungen zur Kunst*, Munich, 1961, p. 37 n. 5, p. 38. For a useful summary of the various theories regarding the production of silhouette papers, see Jake Benson, 'Islamic Methods of Producing Stenciled and "Silhouette" Paper', *Marbling* (Yahoo group), 23 March 2008, https://groups.yahoo.com/neo/groups/marbling/conversations/messages/4566 (accessed June 2015).

3. Richard J. Wolfe, *Marbled Paper: Its History, Techniques, and Patterns*, Philadelphia, 1990, p. 5.

4. For a discussion of the use of stencils in Persian and Mughal manuscripts, see Barbara Brend, *Perspectives on Persian Painting: Illustrations to Amir Khusrau's 'Khamsah'*, London/New York, 2003, p. 240.

5. I am grateful to Susanne Krause for pointing out Emil Kretz's experiments with batik. See Olga Hirsch Collection of Decorated Papers, Folder 49 (J.3615–J.3624), Blockprints: Emil Kretz, Basel (died 1961), British Library, London. See also Marianne Moll, *Emil Kretz und seine Buntpapiere/Emil Kretz and His Decorated Papers*, Hamburg, 2010.

6. J. Ovington, *A Voyage to Suratt, in the Year, 1689. Giving a Large Account of that City …*, London, 1696, pp. 249–50.

7. The Olga Hirsch collection contains many examples of such methods and techniques, including (as categorized by Hirsch) block prints on crêpe paper (J.3494–J.3498), block prints on tissue paper (J.3548), linocuts (J.3244–J.3248, J.2992.a.34-III), roller prints with lithography (J.3175–J.3211) and sprayed papers (Box 27). Olga Hirsch Collection of Decorated Papers, British Library, London.

GLOSSARY

abri
Iranian/Persian term for marbling, meaning 'clouded paper'.

album amicorum
Autograph book made up of blank and decorated paper, popular in northern Europe from the sixteenth to the nineteenth century.

batik paper
Paper decorated by means of the wax-resist method of dyeing textiles.

block-printed paper
Paper printed in one or more colours by hand, using blocks (frequently of wood) into which a design has been cut (the areas intended to show white/plain are excised).

brocade paper
Monochrome or decorated paper with partially embossed metal layer, which is often gold or silver in colour.

bronze varnish paper
Paper that has been block-printed with gold-coloured decoration (the term 'bronze' is used for all metal varnish papers).

carrageenan
Substance derived from seaweed and used in the making of size.

chiyogami
Japanese style of bold and colourful block-printed paper, which first appeared in the seventeenth century (*gami* = 'paper'; *chiyo* = 'very old').

cotton paper
Paper with a chintz design, often floral, as commonly used in the textile industry. The term has largely been replaced by 'block-printed paper', but is still used by some authorities.

crinkled paper
Paper that has been coloured, crinkled up and then flattened again.

dominotier
French term for a maker (or purveyor) of decorated paper.

Dutch gilt
Multi-coloured paper with gold-coloured relief design, often floral. Frequently misused, the term still appears today, but a less ambiguous description is 'brocade paper'.

ebru
Turkish term for marbling, meaning 'cloud'.

embossed paper
Paper decorated in relief (includes brocade paper).

flock paper
Paper pasted with glue and then sprinkled with powdered wool to create a raised design. Reminiscent of velours and velvet.

hatip ebru
Marbling style involving the manipulation of concentric circles with a needle. Named after its inventor, the preacher (or 'hatip') Mehmet Efendi (d. 1773).

lithography
Resist method of printing from a flat surface (traditionally limestone) prepared so that the ink adheres only to the design.

marbled paper
Decorated paper created by placing a sheet of paper on to liquid paint that has been dropped on to a trough or tray of size and arranged into a pattern with the use of brushes, styluses, etc.

paper, coloured
Paper made from dyed pulp.

paper, decorated
Paper decorated on one or both sides after the paper-making process has been completed.

paper, plain
Material made from pulp with no added colourant, i.e. from fibres and water only.

paste paper
Paper covered with coloured paste, which is then manipulated to form a pattern. Has a characteristic texture.

screen-printing
Form of printing where ink is forced through a fine mesh that has been made partially impermeable so as to form an image or pattern on the surface beneath.

silhouette paper
Paper decorated with a clearly defined motif on a patterned background, e.g. a white shape representing a heraldic shield against a background of marbling. Popular in seventeenth-century European autograph books. The precise method is obscure, but was probably similar to stencilling.

size
Marbling base consisting of water made viscous by means of an additive. Used in Turkish and European marbling.

stencilled paper
Paper that has been decorated by placing pre-cut shapes on the surface of the paper and then brushing, wiping or spraying them with paint.

suminagashi
Japanese form of marbling that uses water rather than size as the marbling base (*sumi* = 'ink'; *nagashi* = 'floating').

trickled paper
Paper decorated with dribbles of liquid paint.

For more on the terminology of decorated papers and their identification, see Susanne Krause (ed.), *Buntpapier: ein Bestimmungsbuch/ Decorated Paper: A Guide Book/Sierpapier: een gids*, Hamburg, 2009.

FURTHER READING

BOOKS AND ARTICLES

Paul Adam, *Das Marmorieren des Buchbinders auf Schleimgrund und im Öl- und Kleisterverfahren: nebst Anleitung zum Linoleumschnitt, Schablonierverfahren und Modeldruck für Fachleute und Liebhaber*, 2nd edn, Halle, 1923

Hikmet Barutcugil, *Träume auf Wasser: die türkische Ebrukunst, eine lebendige Tradition/ The Dream of Water: Ebru, the Turkish Art of Marbling: A Living Tradition*, Hamburg, 2012

Anne Chambers, *The Principal Antique Patterns of Marbled Papers*, Burford, 1984

———, *Suminagashi: The Japanese Art of Marbling – A Practical Guide*, London, 1991

Curwen Press, *A Specimen Book of Pattern Papers Designed for and in use at the Curwen Press*, intro. Paul Nash, London, 1928

Decorated Paper Designs 1800/Buntpapier Entwürfe/Les motifs du papier décoré/Design carta decorata/Diseños de papeles pintados: From the Koops-Marcus Collection, Pepin Press Design Series, Amsterdam, 1999

Guido Dessauer, 'Das Buntpapier im 19. Jahrhundert', *International Paper History/ Papiergeschichte international*, vol. 5, no. 1, 1995, pp. 8–12

Marie-Ange Doizy, *De la dominoterie à la marbrure: histoire des techniques traditionelles de la décoration du papier*, Paris, 1996

Yana van Dyke, 'The Art of Marbled Paper: Dynamic Fluids in Flow', *RumiNations* (blog), Metropolitan Museum of Art, 23 June 2015, www.metmuseum.org/about-the-museum/ museum-departments/curatorial-departments/ islamic-art/ruminations/2015/marbled-paper

Phoebe Jane Easton, *Marbling: A History and a Bibliography*, Los Angeles, 1983

Hans Enderli, *Buntpapiere: Geschichte und Rezepte des Buntpapiers mit 205 Original- Buntpapier-Mustern*, Winterthur, 1971

Mirjam Foot, 'The Olga Hirsch Collection of Decorated Papers', *British Library Journal*, vol. 7, no. 1, Spring 1981

Bernd-Ingo Friedrich, 'Ein ganz besonderer Kleister: Herrnhuter Bunt-Papier', *Kulturpixel*, 10 May 2007, www.kulturpixel.de/artikel/8_ Herrnhuter_Papier_Buntpapier_Buchbinderei_ Bruedergemeine_Herrnhut_Zinzendorf

Annabel Teh Gallop with Bernard Arps, *The Golden Letters: Writing Traditions of Indonesia/Surat emas: budaya tulis di Indonesia*, London/Jakarta, 1991

Gefärbt, gekämmt, getunkt, gedruckt: die wunderbare Welt des Buntpapiers (exh. cat.), Mainfränkischen Museum Würzburg, October 2011 – January 2012

Geneviève Guilleminot-Chrétien, *Papiers marbrés français, reliures princières et créations contemporaines* (exh. cat.), Bibliothèque Nationale de France, Paris, November 1987 – January 1988

Albert Haemmerle, *Buntpapier: Herkommen, Geschichte, Techniken, Beziehungen zur Kunst*, Munich, 1977

Josef Halfer, *The Progress of the Marbling Art* [1893], trans. Herman Dieck, New York/ London, 1990

Josef Hauptmann, *De marmerkunst, tot versiering der boeksnede: eene handleiding tot practische beoefening der marmerkunst naar Halfer's Methode* [1899], Dodewaard, 1992

Jan Frederik Heijbroek, *Sierpapier: marmer-, brocaat- en sitspapier in Nederland* (exh. cat.), Rijksmuseum, Amsterdam, November 1994 – February 1995

Ann Herring, *Chiyogami: Hand-Printed Patterned Papers of Japan*, Tokyo/New York, 1987

André Jammes, *Papiers dominotés: trait d'union entre l'imagerie populaire et les papiers peints (France, 1750–1820)*, Paris, 2010

Marian Keyes, 'Decorative End-Papers in the National Art Library in the Victoria and Albert Museum', *The Quarterly*, no. 40, October 2001, pp. 17–24

Christiane F. Kopylov, *Papiers dorés d'Allemagne au siècle des Lumières: suivis de quelques autres papiers décorés (Bilderbogen, Kattunpapiere & Herrnhutpapiere), 1680–1830*, Paris, 2012

Marc Kopylov, *Papiers dominotés français, ou, L'art de revêtir d'éphémères couvertures colorées: livres & brochures entre 1750 et 1820*, Paris, 2012

———, *Papiers dominotés italiens: un univers de couleurs, de fantaisie et d'invention, 1750–1850*, Paris, 2012

Susanne Krause, *Paste Paper/Kleisterpapier*, trans. Susanne Krause and Claire Bolton, Marcham, 2002

———, *Mehr Kleisterpapier/More About Paste Paper*, Hamburg, 2005

——— (ed.), *Buntpapier: ein Bestimmungsbuch/ Decorated Paper: A Guide Book/Sierpapier: een gids*, Hamburg, 2009

Rosamond B. Loring, *Decorated Book Papers: Being an Account of Their Designs and Fashions* [1942], 4th edn, Cambridge, Mass., 2007

Barry McKay (ed.), *Marbling Methods and Receipts from Four Centuries, with Other Instructions useful to Bookbinders*, Kidlington/ New Castle, Del., 1990

Einen Miura, *The Art of Marbled Paper: Marbled Patterns and How to Make Them*, London, 1989

Marianne Moll, *Alte und neue Buntpapiere: Ein Lehr- und Lernbuch*, Hamburg, 2011

John Franklin Mowery and Linda Hohneke, *The Valerian and Laura Lada-Mocarski Decorated Paper Collection*, Washington DC, 1998

Iris Nevins, *Varieties of Spanish Marbling: A Handbook of Practical Instruction with Twelve Original Marbled Samples*, North Hills, Pa., 1991

Dag-Ernst Petersen, *Gebunden in der Dampfbuchbinderei: Buchbinden im Wandel des 19. Jahrhunderts*, Wiesbaden, 1994

Piccarda Quilici, *Carte decorate nella legatoria del '700: dalle raccolte della Biblioteca casanatense*, Rome, 1988

Gisela Reschke – Buntpapier: Tradition und Gegenwart (exh. cat.), Gutenberg-Museum Mainz, July–September 2007

Frieder Schmidt, 'Buntpapier in den Sammlungen des Deutschen Buch- und Schriftmuseums', *Deutschen Buch- und Schriftmuseums*, http://d-nb.info/1026682312/34

Hans Schmoller, *Chinese Decorated Papers*, Newton, Pa., 1987

Tanya Schmoller, *To Brighten Things Up: The Schmoller Collection of Decorated Papers*, Manchester, 2008

Jean-Pierre Seguin, *Dominos: papiers imprimés*, Paris, 1991

Nedim Sönmez, *Ebru: Marmorpapiere*, Ravensburg, 1992

Nedim Sönmez and Yvonne Jäckle-Sönmez, *Türkisch Papier/Ebru/Turkish Marbled Paper*, Tübingen, 1987

Antonio Vélez Celemín, *El Marmoleado: del papel guardas obra arte*, Madrid, 2012

Victoria and Albert Museum, *The Victoria and Albert Colour Books: Decorative Endpapers*, London, 1985

Voornamelijk papier: een papieren spiegelbeeld van Henk Voorn bij zijn afscheid als conservator van de afdeling Papierhistorie van de Koninklijke Bibliotheek (exh. cat.), National Library of the Netherlands, The Hague, 1986

Richard J. Wolfe, *Marbled Paper: Its History, Techniques, and Patterns*, Philadelphia, 1990

Charles W. Woolnough, *The Whole Art of Marbling as Applied to Paper, Book-Edges, etc.*, London, 1881

ONLINE RESOURCES

Bibliothèque et Archives du Château de Chantilly
www.bibliotheque-conde.fr/expositions/histoire-de-la-reliure/papiers-de-garde-dores-de-la-bibliotheque-du-chateau-de-chantilly
Examples of brocade papers from the chateau's library.

Bibliothèque des Arts Décoratifs, Paris
www.bibliothequedesartsdecoratifs.com/consultation/pdf/M5053JO2009Xo000002.pdf
Illustrated essay describing different types of decorated paper.

Bibliothèque Nationale de France, Picture Collection
http://images.bnf.fr
Features examples of decorated papers.

British Library, Olga Hirsch Collection of Decorated Papers
www.bl.uk
Further information about the collection may be found on the library's website.

Buntpapier.eu
www.buntpapier.eu/buntpapierarten
Various examples of paste papers.

Buntpapier.org
www.buntpapier.org
Website devoted to decorated-paper research.

Conservation Online
http://cool.conservation-us.org/don
An online dictionary of bookbinding terminology, including decorated-paper terms.

Deutsche National Bibliothek, Historical Paper Collections
www.dnb.de/EN/DBSM/Bestaende/PapierhistSammlung/papierhistsammlung_node.html

Ligatus (University of the Arts London)
www.ligatus.org.uk/node/718
Currently helping to develop a digital tool for the identification of decorated papers.

Manchester Metropolitan University Library, Image Collection Website
http://ibs001.colo.firstnet.net.uk/mmu/index.php
Features digitized decorated papers from the Schmoller Collection of Decorated Papers.

National Library of the Netherlands
www.kb.nl/en/resources-research-guides/kb-collections/bookbindings-and-paper-history/paper-historical-collection
A collection of digitized decorated papers.

Spanish Ministry of Education, Culture and Sport
http://en.www.mcu.es/archivos/MC/EncuaderArtist/PapelesPin.html
Examples of different decorated-paper techniques.

Turkish Cultural Foundation
www.turkishculture.org/fine-art/visual-arts/marbling/turkish-marbling-ebru-564.htm?type=1
Description of Turkish marbling with examples.

'Under the Covers: The Hidden Art of Endpapers'
http://salemathenaeum.net/exhibition-1
Online version of an exhibition at the Salem Athenaeum, Salem, Mass.

Victoria and Albert Museum, London
http://collections.vam.ac.uk
Examples of decorated end-leaves held by the museum may be found using its 'Search the Collections' website.

INDEX

Page numbers in *italic* refer to illustrations.

A

A. Mame et Cie 100, *100*
Akbar, Emperor 206
albums *16*, 21; *album amicorum* 206, 237
Amman, Jost *206*
art nouveau *172*, 221, 236
Arts and Crafts Movement 63
Aschaffenburg 22, 172, *172*, 197
Augsburg 11, 16, 99, 100, 101, 112, 113, 122
Ayres, Alfred *173*

B

Bache, B. F. *11*
Baskerville, John *10*, 11
Bassano 11, 13, 152
batik 16, 206, *207*
Bawden, Edward 18, 172
Behrens, Lilli 65, *67*
Berlin, Isaiah 18
Berlin Secession 179
Bewick, Thomas 14
Bilderbogen 100
bingata 246
block printing 9, 11–14, 15, 18, 19, 99, 133–69, *209*, 215, 228, 233; *see also chiyogami*
book covers 15, 197, *201*, 232
brocade papers 9, 12–16, 18, *19*, 99, 99–131; *see also Bilderbogen*
bronze varnish papers 99, 133, *134*
Buntpapierfabrik AG 22
Büttner, Erich *178*, 179, *179*, *192–3*, 193, 197, *201*, 202

C

Cai Lun 10
calligraphy 21, *208*
Chaloner, William 22
chiyogami 14, 16, 133–4, *135*, *140*, *141*, *148*, *151*, *152*, *155*, *158*, *164*
Cissarz, Johann Vincenz 227, *229*, 232, *232*, *233*, 236, *236*
Cockerell, Sydney (Sandy) 18, 50; & Son *49*, 59, *61*, 172
cotton papers 16, 168
Curwen Press 18, 172, *173*, *194*, 196

D

Dackerman, Susan 17
d'Alembert, Jean 30
Day, Graham *57*, 58
decorating techniques, miscellaneous 204–46

Derome family 11
Dessauer, Alois *171*
Diderot, Denis 30
dissertations 63, 99
dominotiers 13, 14
Doves Press 39
Dresden 227
Dürer, Albrecht 17
Düsseldorf 65
'Dutch gilt' 9, 99, *99*
Düzgünman, Mustafa 22

E

Eckart, Johann Georg 116, *116*
Efendi, Hatip Mehmed 13, 22
Efendi, Şeyh Sadık 13
Elizabeth I, Queen 14
embossing *221*, 227, *244*, 248, *249*
Enderlin, Anna Barbara 99
Enderlin, Jacob 99
end-leaves 11, 15, 30, 40, 51, 99, *172*, 179, 197, *201*, *205*
Ernst, Otto 193
Evelyn, John 11, 16

F

'fancy' paper 13, 205
Faraday, Michael 22
FitzRoy, Robert *18*
flocking 205, 206, *212*
Florence 11, 136
Foot, Mirjam 22, 106
Frankfurt am Main 70, 71, 76, 82, 95
Franklin, Benjamin 11, 12
Franks, Catherine *172*
Fraser, Claud Lovat *173*
Fraser, James H. 63
Freise, Dorothea *36–7*, 38
Fröhlich, Mathias 100
Fürth 13, 107, 122
Fuzuli 17

G

G. N. & Abel Renner *14*
G. W. Gwynne & Sons 39, *41*
Ghys, Jean-Baptiste 158, *158–9*, *161*, 162
Giannini & Son 136, *136*
Goethe, Johann Wolfgang von 14
Grantchester 18
greetings cards 16
Griselini, Francesco 142

H

Haemmerle, Albert 9, 168
Haichele, Simon 113
Halfer, Joseph 22, 44
Hall, Victoria 21, *80*, 82
Hauptmann, Josef 44

Herring, Ann 134
Herrnhut 63, 88
Heyden, Jacob van der 205
Hiroba family 15
Hirsch, Olga 9, 11, *21*, 30, 122, 215, 237, 246; *see also* Olga Hirsch collection
Hirsch, Renate 69, 70, 71, *74–5*, 76, *79*, *81*, 82, 95, *95*
Holme, Charles 95
Hupp, Otto 221, *222*

I

invitations 16
Irmler, Annemarie *219*, 220

J

journals 16
Jugendstil see art nouveau

K

katagami 16, *16*, 206, *240*, *241*
katazome 246
Kersten, Paul 22, *42–3*, 44, *48*, 50, 51, *51*, 59, *59*, 71, *73*, 83, *84*, *86*, *87*, 88, 92, *93*, 95, *96–7*, 172, *172*, 196, 197, *197*, 199, *212–13*, 214, 221, *223*
Kornicki, Peter 10
Krause, Suzanne 17
Kretz, Emil 206, *207*
Kretzer, Max 197
Kyster, Anker 31

L

Lautenbacher, Karl 209
Lechner, Johann *13*, 122
Leopold, Johann Friedrich *12*, 122
letterpress papers *171*
linings for chests and cases 13, 14, 15
lithography 11, *17*, 134, 171, *171*, *173*, *184*, *185*, *186*, *187*, *192–3*, *194*, 196, *198*, 201, 202, 210, *211*, 215, 224, *225*, *226*, 228, *229*, *230*, *231*, *232*, *233*, 236, *238*, *242–3*
London 13, 22, 39, 205
Ludwig, Eduard 88, *90*, *91*
Luther, Martin 13

M

Mack family 17
Mandelbrot, Benoit 18
marbling 8–13, 15–19, 21–61, *174–5*, *176*, *181*, *182*, 197, *199*, 203, 205, 237; bench (Morris) 24, *25*; bouquet 9, 22; comb 22, *28*, *41*, 44, *45*, *49*, *56*, 60, *61*, *180*; curl 22; Dutch 22; *hatip ebru* 13; lead shot 38; moiré *34–5*, 200; nonpareil 22; peacock 22; Persian 12; shell 22, *29*; snail 22, *52–3*; Spanish 10, 22, *183*, *188–9*; stone 22, *195*; Stormont 22, *203*;

sunspot (tiger eye) 22, *50*; Turkish 12, 19, 21, *23*, 24, *54–5*; veined 22; *see also suminagashi*
mass production 170–203
Maziarczyk, Claire 64
Mehrer, David *110*, 112
Merktl, Mattheus 113, *114*
Meyer, Johann Wilhelm 122
Mieser, Abraham 113
Milano, Alberto 162
Mitsuhiro, Karasumaru 10
Miura, Tini 18
Morris, E. W. 24
Motesiczky, Marie-Louise von 227
Munck, Johann Carl 101, *102*, 113
Munck, Johann Michael 122
music scores 63, *64*, 99

N

Nash, Paul 18, 172
Nuremberg 11, *14*, 17, 99, 100, 106, 116, 117

O

Okyay, Necmettin *21*, 22
Olga Hirsch collection 9, 101
Ovington, J. 207

P

Padeloup family 11
paper currency *11*, 12, 13
papiers dominotés 9
Papillon family 15; Jean-Michel 18
Paris 11, *12*, 13, 15, 18
paste papers *63*, 63–95
Pepys, Samuel 15–16
picotage 133
playing cards, backing for 13

R

Ravilious, Eric *17*, 18, 172
Ravilious, Tirzah 45, *45*
Reimund, Paul *100*, 116, 117, *117*, *120*, 122
Remondini family 13, 133; firm 152; Giuseppe 13
Renner & Abel 106, *106*, *107*
Renvoize, Frederick Reni 13
Réveillon, Jean-Baptiste 13; workshop *12*, 15
roller printing 215
Ruette, Macé 11
Rumi 13

S

Salter, Rebecca 10
Salto, Axel 184, *184*, 185, *185*, 186, *186*, 187, *187*
Schindler, Johann Paul 107, *109*
Schmoller, Tanya 11

Schwibecher, Johann Michael *100*
scrapbooks 16, *21*
screen-printing 134, 172
Senefelder, Alois 171
Seymour, Edward 205
Shah Jahan 21
silhouette papers 15, 16, *205*, 206
silk-screen printing 215
slipcases 15, *16*
sprinkling 11, *56*, 58, 205, *218*
stencilling 15–16, 99, *108*, *121*, 206, *206*, 212, 219, 225, 237; *see also katagami*; *katazome*
Stoy, Georg Christoph 99–100, 113, *115*, 122
Su-I-chien 10
suminagashi 10, 15, 21, *21*
Sutherland, Graham 18, 172, 196, *196*

T

Tours 100

W

wallpaper 15, 206; *see also* flocking
Wiener Werkstätte 177, *177*
Wolfe, Richard J. 59, 206
woodblock printing *see* block printing
Woodcock, John *194*, 196
Woolnough, Charles 11, 19, 31, 51
wrappers *113*, *139*; book 13, 15; foodstuff 9, *14*, *14*, 205
wrapping paper 16, 18
writing paper 16, 205

PICTURE ACKNOWLEDGMENTS

Page 6: Rosamond B. Loring; pages 36–7: Dorothea Freise; page 45: © Estate of Tirzah Ravilious. All rights reserved, DACS 2015; pages 49, 61: Sydney (Sandy) Cockerell/ Cockerell & Son; page 57: © Graham Day; pages 69, 70–1, 74–5, 79, 81, 95: Renate Hirsch; page 194: John Woodcock; page 196: © Estate of Graham Sutherland; page 207: Emil Kretz